641.8653 MACG SE

MacGregor, Elaine.

Quick to decorate cakes
15x 12/05 LT 8/05
88-5-97

STOCKTON-SAN JOAQUIN COUNTY LIBRARY
D0568232

WITHDRAWN

Quick
to
Decorate
Cakes

QUICK TO DECORATE CAKES

Elaine MacGregor

MEREHURST PRESS
LONDON

Important: use only one set of measurements. The quantities given in metric are not always exact conversions of the imperial measurements. Cup conversions of imperial measurements are given below.

Imperial	Cups
5 fl oz liquid	⅔ cup
10 fl oz liquid	1¼ cups
20 fl oz liquid	2½ cups
40 fl oz liquid	5 cups
1lb granulated or caster (superfine) sugar	2 cups
1lb brown sugar	2 cups
1lb icing (confectioner's) sugar	3½ cups
1lb butter	2 cups
1lb flour	4 cups
1lb dried fruit	3 cups
8oz glacé cherries	1 cup
4oz chopped nuts	1 cup
4oz cocoa powder	1 cup
1oz flour	¼ cup
1oz granulated or caster (superfine) sugar	2 tablespoons
1oz butter	2 tablespoons

I would like to thank my husband Stuart, who does such a lot of work on these books, my children Christopher and Fiona, who are my sternest critics, and to all my staff at Woodnutt's for their help. E.M.

Published 1988 by Merehurst Press
5 Great James Street
London WC1N 3DA

© Copyright 1988 Merehurst Limited

Co-published in Australia and New Zealand
by Child & Associates,
9 Clearview Place, Brookvale, Sydney 2100.

ISBN 0 948075 81 3

All rights reserved. No part of this publication may be reproduced, stored in a retrieval system, or transmitted in any form or by any means, electronic, mechanical, photocopying, recording or otherwise, without the prior written permission of the copyright owner.

Managing Editor Alison Leach
Designer Dave Copsey
Photographer Graham Tann, assisted by Yolande Salisbury and Lucy Baker
Typeset by London Composition Ltd, London SE1.
Colour Separation by Fotographics Ltd, London-Hong Kong
Printed by Henri Proost, Turnhout, Belgium

CONTENTS

FOREWORD

Many years ago I had the opportunity to work in Australia. I went there to give demonstrations of cookery on television and to live audiences. It was a wonderful experience, not only because I loved the country and the people, but because it gave me the opportunity to appreciate the skills of cooks in Australia.

The thing that impressed me above all else was the incredibly high standard of sugarcraft and cake decoration which was done in ways I had not met before. As you may well imagine I made quite certain I learned these techniques before returning to Britain.

When Elaine MacGregor came to Britain and established her school of cake decoration in the neighbourhood in which I live, I went to meet her and wish her success in her enterprise. I realised that her skill in sugarcraft is almost unbelievable and the manner in which she decorates cakes supremely artistic. Since our first meeting Elaine has gone from strength to strength; her classes are known throughout Britain and she visits other countries too.

I think the most important part of her work is the way in which she inspires other people to emulate her. Cake decoration is a wonderfully satisfying art and Elaine's pupils would stress the pleasure they have derived from developing their skills.

Elaine is a very practical lady snd she realises there are many, many people who want to achieve a good standard of workmanship within a relatively short time. This book will help achieve this; in fact it will be invaluable. I wish it, and the author, great success.

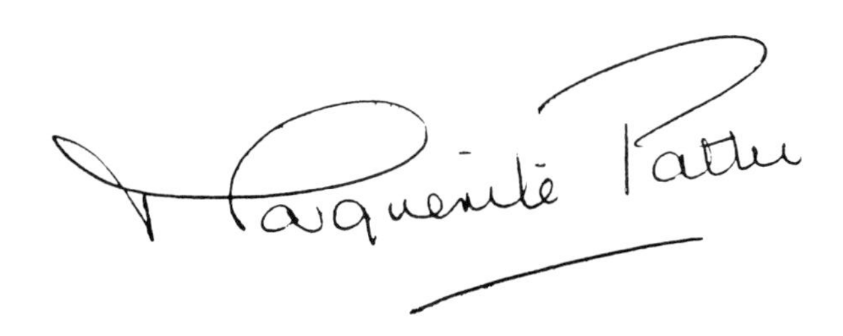

INTRODUCTION

We frequently overhear people standing beside our window looking at the varied display cakes made at our cake decorating school, remark, 'I'll have to buy a cake again, I just don't have time to make one.'

It is true that practised hands can work more quickly than those that are less experienced, but almost anyone can decorate a cake. With a little imagination and only a minimum of equipment, it is surprisingly easy to create cakes suitable for a wide variety of occasions without spending too much time or money.

Each of the cakes illustrated in this book can be decorated in under two hours, and many of them can be completed in less than half of that time. The vital ingredients for success are imagination and a little planning. If these are combined with some of the ideas shown and the information given, you will gain far more satisfaction than it is possible to derive from merely choosing a cake with pink icing or one with blue icing. It is hoped that the imaginative shapes and many original designs in this book will be a positive encouragement to all busy people to acquire the creative and sometimes spectacular skills of cake decorating.

Elaine MacGregor

□CAKE RECIPES□

Rich Fruit Cake

Ingredients
225g (8oz) sultanas
225g (8oz) currants
225g (8oz) raisins
125g (4oz) glacé cherries, halved
50g (2oz) mixed citrus peel, chopped
50g (2oz) almonds, unblanched and cut
125ml (4fl oz) sherry or brandy
225g (8oz) plain (all-purpose) flour
50g (2oz) self-raising flour
5ml (1 tsp) mixed spice
5ml (1 tsp) cinnamon
1ml (¼ tsp) grated nutmeg
5ml (1 tsp) salt
225g (8oz) butter
225g (8oz) soft dark brown sugar
4 eggs

Equipment
1 22.5-cm (9-in) round or 20-cm (8-in) square cake tin (pan), greased and lined (see method)
double thickness of brown paper
mixing bowls
sieve
wooden spoon or electric mixer
metal whisk
large metal spoon
fine skewer

Put the sultanas, currants, raisins, glacé cherries, mixed citrus peel and almonds in a bowl. Moisten with the sherry or brandy, cover and leave overnight.

Heat the oven to 220°C (425°F) Gas Mark 7. Line the tin (pan) with a double thickness of brown paper on its base and a single thickness around its side. Sift together the flours, spices and salt, and put to one side in a separate bowl. Cream together the butter and sugar until light and fluffy – this should take about 10 minutes, or 5 minutes if using an electric mixer. Lightly beat the eggs, then add to the creamed mixture a little at a time, beating well between each addition and adding some sifted flour to prevent the mixture curdling. Fold in the remaining flour and the fruit mixture alternately and stir carefully until all the ingredients are thoroughly mixed. Turn the mixture into the prepared tin, smoothing the top with the back of a metal spoon and making a shallow depression in the centre. Reduce the oven temperature to 150°C (300°F) Gas Mark 2 and bake the cake for 2½-3 hours, checking the cake 30 minutes before it is due to be removed from the oven. To test if the cake is cooked, insert a fine skewer into the centre. If it comes out clean, the cake is cooked. Remove from the oven and leave the cake to cool in the tin.

Variations
Use equal quantities of sherry and brandy, or replace the alcohol with orange juice.

Light Fruit Cake

Ingredients
225g (8oz) mixed dried fruit
125ml (4fl oz) orange juice or sherry
225g (8oz) butter or margarine
225g (8oz) caster (superfine) sugar
3 eggs
225g (8oz) plain (all-purpose) flour, sifted

Equipment
1 22.5-cm (9-in) round or 20-cm (8-in) square cake tin (pan), greased and lined
mixing bowls
wooden spoon or electric mixer
metal whisk
large metal spoon
fine skewer

Put the dried fruit in a bowl and moisten with the orange juice or sherry. Cover and leave overnight.

Heat the oven to 160°C (325°F) Gas Mark 3. Cream together the butter or margarine and sugar until light and fluffy – this should take about 10 minutes, or 5 minutes if using an electric mixer. Lightly beat the eggs, then add to the creamed mixture a little at a time, beating well between each addition and adding some sifted flour to prevent the mixture curdling. Fold in the remaining flour and the fruit mixture alternately and stir carefully until all the ingredients are thoroughly mixed. Turn the mixture into the prepared tin (pan), smoothing the top with the back of a metal spoon.

Bake the cake for 2-2½ hours, checking the cake 30 minutes before it is due to be removed from the oven. To test if the cake is cooked, insert a fine skewer into the centre. If it comes out clean, the cake is cooked. Remove from the oven and leave the cake to cool in the tin.

Madeira Cake

Ingredients
350g (12oz) unsalted butter or margarine
350g (12oz) caster (superfine) sugar
4 large eggs
350g (12oz) self-raising flour, sifted
175g (6oz) plain (all-purpose) flour
5ml (1 tsp) lemon juice
about 30ml (2 tbsp) milk
caster (superfine) sugar for sprinkling

Equipment
1 25-cm (10-in) round or 22.5-cm (9-in) square cake tin (pan), greased and lined
mixing bowls
wooden spoon or electric mixer
metal whisk
sieve
large metal spoon
wire cooling rack
sheet of greaseproof paper

Heat the oven to 180°C (350°) Gas Mark 4. Cream together the butter or margarine and sugar until light and fluffy – this should take about 15 minutes, or 8 minutes if using an electric mixer. Lightly beat the eggs, then add to the creamed mixture a little at a time, following each addition with 15ml (1 tbsp) of the self-raising flour. Sift the remaining self-raising flour with the plain (all-purpose) flour and fold into the creamed mixture, stirring carefully until the ingredients are thoroughly mixed. Add the lemon juice and just enough milk to give the mixture a soft, dropping consistency. Turn the mixture into the prepared tin (pan) and smooth the top with the back of a metal spoon, indenting the centre slightly. Bake the cake for 1½ hours or until risen and golden brown on top and springy to the touch. Remove from the oven and leave the cake to cool in the tin on the wire rack for 5 minutes, then turn out on to a sheet of greaseproof paper sprinkled with caster (superfine) sugar and remove the lining paper.

Calculating quantities

It is quite easy to obtain an idea of the approximate weight of rich fruit cake mixture you need to fill different sizes and shapes of tins (pans). Simply fill the tin with water to the depth you would expect to fill it with cake mixture, then weigh it. Subtract the weight of the tin itself and you are left with the approximate weight of the mixture you will need. You don't have to be too accurate – you can round the amount up or down to give you a weight from which the recipe quantities can be calculated. The proportions of the ingredients must remain the same as those given in the cake recipes. Remember to adjust the length of the baking time – a 32.5-cm (13-in) round rich fruit cake, for example, will need about 6 hours.

As several of the rich fruit cakes in this book are baked in round or square tins, the following chart provides a useful guide.

Cake tin (pan) size	Average weight of cake mixture
15-cm (6-in) round 12.5-cm (5-in) square	950g (2lb 2 oz)
17.5-cm (7-in) round 15-cm (6-in) square	1.1kg (2lb 8 oz)
20-cm (8-in) round 17.5-cm (7-in) square	1.8kg (4lb)
22.5-cm (9-in) round 20-cm (8-in) square	2.8kg (6lb)
25-cm (10-in) round 22.5-cm (9-in) square	3.6kg (8lb)
30-cm (12-in) round 27.5-cm (11-in) square	5.6kg (12lb 8oz)
32.5-cm (13-in) round 30-cm (12-in) square	7.2kg (16lb)

☐ ICING RECIPES ☐

Sugarpaste

Ingredients
25g (1oz) powdered gelatine
300ml (10 fl oz) water
450g (1lb) granulated sugar
125ml (4 fl oz) liquid glucose
30ml (6 tsp) glycerine
5ml (1 tsp) cream of tartar
125g (4 oz) white vegetable fat
1.4kg (3lb) icing (confectioner's) sugar, sifted

Equipment
mixing bowls
small saucepan
wide, heavy-based saucepan
wooden spoon
pastry brush
sugar thermometer
cup
air-tight container

Sprinkle the gelatine over half the water in a small bowl and leave to soften for 2-3 minutes. Stand the bowl in a saucepan of hot water and stir until dissolved and quite hot. Put the granulated sugar, liquid glucose, glycerine, cream of tartar and remaining water in a wide, heavy-based saucepan over a medium heat. Stir until every grain of sugar has dissolved, then bring to the boil. Using a pastry brush dipped in cold water, remove any sugar crystals from the side of the pan. Cook over a high heat until the sugar thermometer shows 150°C (240°F). Remove from the heat and place the saucepan in a bowl of cold water to prevent any more cooking. Leave to cool for 3-4 minutes and then stir in the white vegetable fat and the dissolved gelatine. Add the icing (confectioner's) sugar a cupful at a time, mixing well between each addition to ensure a smooth paste. Store in an air-tight container for 24 hours before using. If necessary, knead in extra icing sugar to obtain the required consistency.

Pastillage

Ingredients
10ml (2 tsp) powdered gelatine
25ml (5 tsp) water
450g (1lb) icing (confectioner's) sugar, sifted
15ml (3 tsp) gum tragacanth
10ml (2 tsp) liquid glucose
10ml (2 tsp) white vegetable fat
1 egg white

Equipment
mixing bowls
electric mixer
saucepan

Soak the gelatine in the water for about 30 minutes. Put the icing (confectioner's) sugar and gum tragacanth in the bowl of an electric mixer over a saucepan of hot water. Dissolve the liquid glucose, white vegetable fat and gelatine over a very low heat – a bowl of hot water is adequate. When the sugar is warm to the touch, put the bowl back on the mixer and having warmed the beater, turn on to slow speed. Add the liquid glucose mixture and the egg white. Increase the speed to maximum and beat for about 15 minutes. The longer and harder the pastillage is beaten, the whiter it will look.

Petal paste

Ingredients
15ml (3 tsp) water
150g (5oz) Woodnutt's petal paste powder

Equipment
small mixing bowl
sieve
wooden spoon

The unique 'instant' petal paste powder is available from specialist cake decorating shops. It is a mixture of sugar and edible gums, and only needs the addition of liquid to make a pastillage.

Put the water into a small bowl and sieve 100g (3½oz) of the petal paste powder into the water, stirring well until the powder is completely blended. Cover the bowl and leave for 5 minutes. Sift the remaining powder on to a clean flat surface. Knead the paste thoroughly into the powder until the mixture is smooth and elastic. For more plasticity, add a little white vegetable fat – about the size of a small pea – to the finished paste. Store the paste in an air-tight container. It can be used immediately but, for best results, it should be left for 24 hours.

Royal icing

Ingredients
1 egg white
350g (12oz) icing (confectioner's) sugar, sifted
few drops lemon juice

Equipment
mixing bowl
palette knife

Put the egg white in a completely grease-free bowl. Use a palette knife to break up the egg white. Very gradually add the icing (confectioner's) sugar, about a teaspoonful at a time, working it into the egg white. Beat very thoroughly with the palette knife between each addition. If you don't beat enough, the finished icing will have a dull, grainy texture. Add a few drops of lemon juice to whiten the icing and improve its strength. The icing should have a smooth, creamy texture. If you are coating a cake, the icing should be stiff enough to stand in soft peaks, but it should be much stiffer for piping shells, for example. If it is too stiff, adjust the consistency with a few drops of water. If it is too runny, add more icing sugar.

Buttercream

Ingredients
125g (4oz) unsalted butter, softened
175g (6oz) icing (confectioner's) sugar, sifted
few drops vanilla or lemon essence

Equipment
mixing bowl
wooden spoon or electric mixer

Put the butter in a warmed bowl and beat until it is light and fluffy. Add the icing (confectioner's) sugar a little at a time, beating well between each addition. Beat in the vanilla or lemon essence. Transfer to a covered container and store for up to one week in the fridge. Bring the buttercream to room temperature before using.

Variations
Chocolate Blend 15ml (1 tbsp) cocoa with 15ml (1 tbsp) hot water to give a smooth paste. Beat into the buttercream.
Coffee Dissolve 5ml (1 tsp) instant coffee in 10ml (2 tsp) hot water. Beat into the buttercream.

Marzipan

Ingredients
450g (1lb) granulated sugar
150ml (5 fl oz) plus 60ml (4 tbsp) water
large pinch cream of tartar
350g (12oz) ground almonds
2 egg whites
icing (confectioner's) sugar, sifted
almond essence (optional)

Equipment
large saucepan
metal spoon
sugar thermometer

Place the sugar and water in a large saucepan and heat very gently, stirring with a metal spoon. Do not allow the syrup to boil until every grain of sugar has dissolved. Add the cream of tartar and bring the syrup to the boil, then boil rapidly without stirring until it reaches the soft ball stage – 110°-115°C (230°-240°F) on a sugar thermometer. Do not overboil, or the icing will thicken and be crumbly to handle. To test for soft ball, drop a small teaspoonful of the syrup into a cup of cold water – it should form a soft ball when rubbed between the fingers. Stop the syrup boiling by placing the base of the saucepan in cold water, then immediately stir in the ground almonds and unbeaten egg whites. Return the pan to a low heat and stir until the mixture thickens slightly. Turn the mixture out on to a marble slab, plastic laminated surface or wooden board, and work it until it cools and thickens. When it is cool enough, knead the mixture with your hands until it is smooth, using a light dusting of sifted icing (confectioner's) sugar. It will take up to half its weight in icing sugar, but if a lot of sugar is used, some almond essence must be added. Store in an air-tight jar or thick plastic bag until required. If it dries out, moisten with a little egg white. This recipe makes 900g (2lb) of marzipan; the quantities can be doubled, if necessary.

□USING SUGARPASTE□

Many of the cakes shown in this book are covered with sugarpaste *(see page 10)*, which is also known as rolled fondant. Its main advantage over royal icing is that it can be used to cover a cake in a single step. Sugarpaste can also be bought ready-made, from some supermarkets and most specialist cake decoration shops.

Colouring sugarpaste

If you intend to colour the sugarpaste, first work out how much you will need for the entire cake and colour the full quantity before dividing it. This way, you will ensure that the icing of each part will be of exactly the same colour.

Colour sugarpaste with specially made concentrated food colours, not the highly diluted liquids which are sold by most supermarkets. Dip a skewer or cocktail stick (wooden toothpick) into the colour, and draw it across the paste, wiping the colour from the skewer. Then knead the fondant as if it were bread dough, to distribute the colour. Add more colour if required.

Check that the colour is thoroughly blended by cutting the fondant into two pieces with a clean knife. If it is full of deeper-coloured lines and swirls, continue to knead it. Test again and this time the fondant should be evenly coloured.

Rolling out sugarpaste

When either colouring sugarpaste or rolling it out, dust the flat surface with just enough sifted icing (confectioner's) sugar to prevent the sugarpaste from sticking – too much will make the icing dry out, which will lead to cracking as it is applied to the cake. Never use cornflour (cornstarch) to dust the surface, as it may encourage fermentation underneath the icing after it has been applied to the cake.

If you are making a tiered cake, divide the fondant into the correct proportions for each section. Keep the portions you are not using immediately closely covered in plastic wrap and as air-tight as possible.

Roll out the sugarpaste, giving it a half-turn at intervals, until it is sufficiently large to cover the top and sides of the cake.

Covering the cake

Brush a little alcohol or water all over a marzipanned cake to make a good bond for the sugarpaste. Alcohol helps to sterilise the surface and improves the flavour. Rum, brandy or sherry are suitable for this purpose, but you can use isopropyl alcohol which is obtainable in small quantities from chemists.

Pick up the icing, supporting it with the palms of your hands and forearms. Lay it over the cake, with the edge of the icing touching the flat surface on the far side. Carefully slide one hand out from under the icing and use it to mould the fondant gently against the back of the cake. Slowly withdraw the other hand, taking care not to stretch the icing or make a hole in it and smoothing the fondant against the top of the cake as you do so. Make sure that you do not trap air under the surface.

If the cake has corners, flare the icing and mould it on to the corners first. It is easy to avoid creating any folds or pleats if you use the soft part of your palm to 'stroke' the icing into place.

Then smooth the icing against the sides and trim off any excess around the base with a sharp knife. A really even and glossy surface can be achieved by 'polishing' the icing with a large plastic smoother. Use a smaller one, or a cake smoother with a bevelled edge, to flatten the sides and neaten the top edges and corners.

If you notice an air pocket or bubble under the icing, prick it with a pin, held at an angle, force out the air and smooth the icing again to remove any trace of the pin-hole. Use a pin with a large coloured head, since it is easy to see. It can be very worrying if you can't find the pin you used when you are cleaning up later, making you wonder whether it has been buried in the icing!

Placing a cake on its board

The easiest way to secure a cake to its board is to put a small cone of moistened sugarpaste in the centre of the board. Pick up the cake by sliding it off the edge of the flat surface on to the palm of your hand and hold it over the board. Quickly withdraw your hand, allowing the cake to drop on to the board. Use the smoother to press down the cake, flattening the sugarpaste cone. Be careful not to leave any fingerprints on the newly iced cake.

Decorating

If you wish to decorate using embossing tools or crimpers, this must be done within 30 minutes of covering the cake, while the icing is still soft. Otherwise the surface will have begun to harden and will crack under the pressure of the decorating tools when you try to use them.

Covering a cake with sugarpaste

If you are not experienced, you will find that either round or oval cakes are easier to cover as there are no corners.

Use the same technique for applying marzipan if you are covering a cake with sugarpaste.

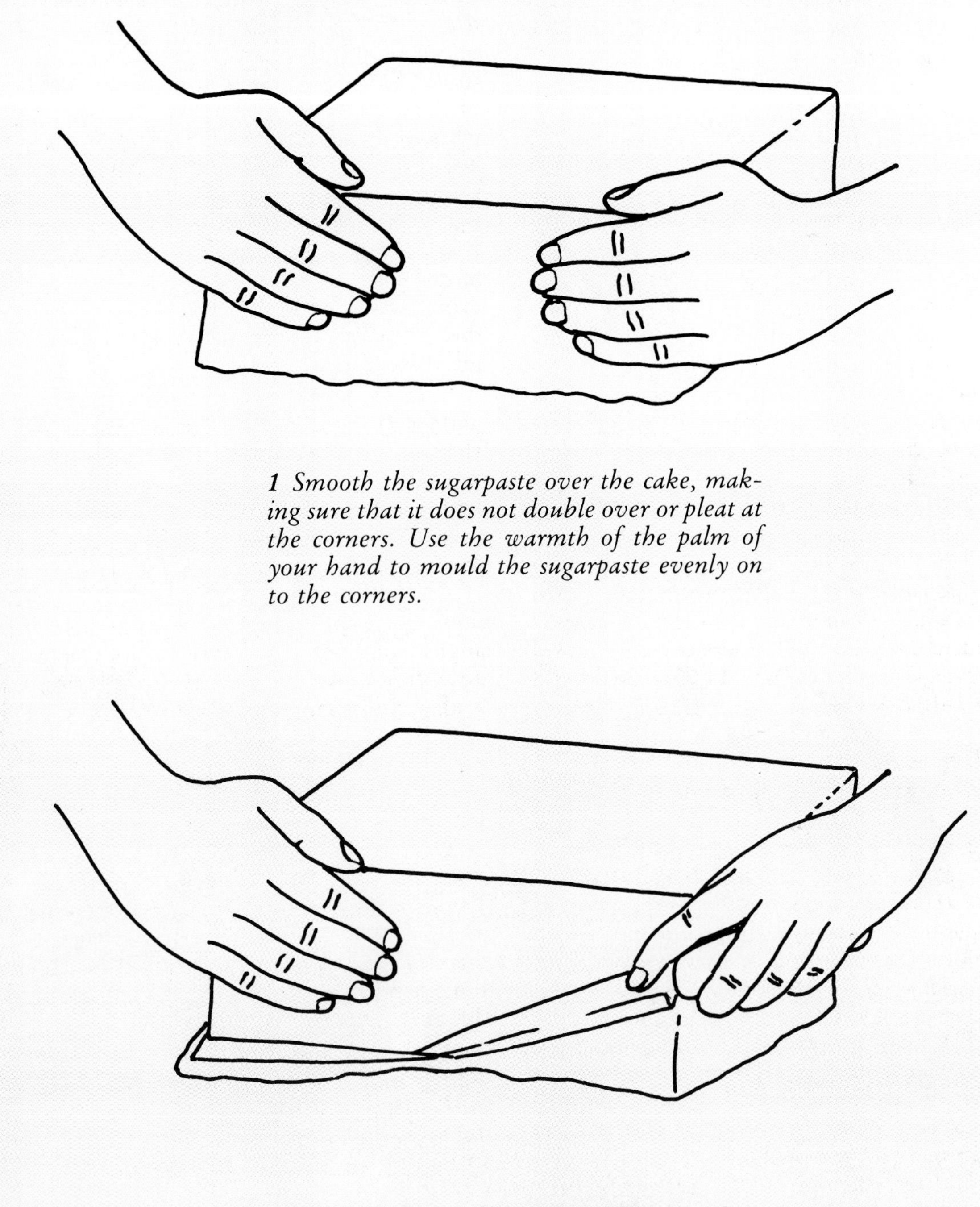

1 Smooth the sugarpaste over the cake, making sure that it does not double over or pleat at the corners. Use the warmth of the palm of your hand to mould the sugarpaste evenly on to the corners.

2 Cut off the excess sugarpaste with a sharp knife before placing the cake on its board.

Make piping bags in high grade vegetable parchment paper for delicate piping work such as scrolls, lines or lettering. Most grades of greaseproof and waxed paper are not strong enough and often split during use. Larger piping bags can be made from triangles measuring 40 x 32.5 x 25cm (16 x 13 x 10in).

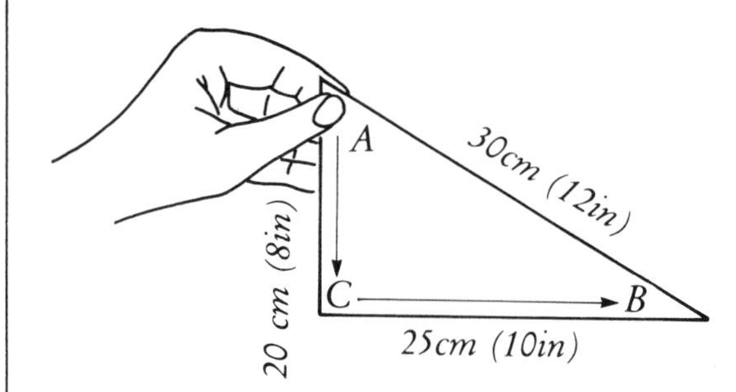

1 Mark the triangle with the arrows and letters as shown. Hold the triangle in your left hand, between the index finger and thumb at point A with the longest side of the triangle uppermost.

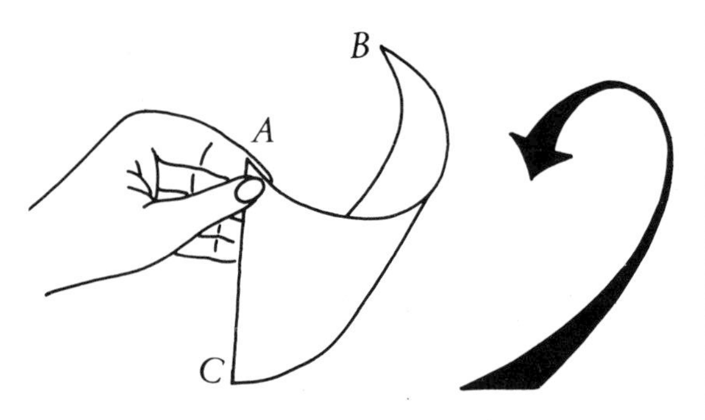

2 Hold point B in your right hand, take point B away from you and wrap it over the back of the fingers of your left hand.

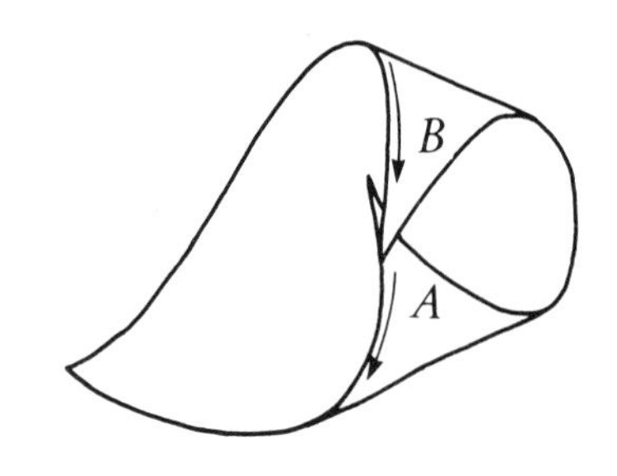

3 Place point B over point A.

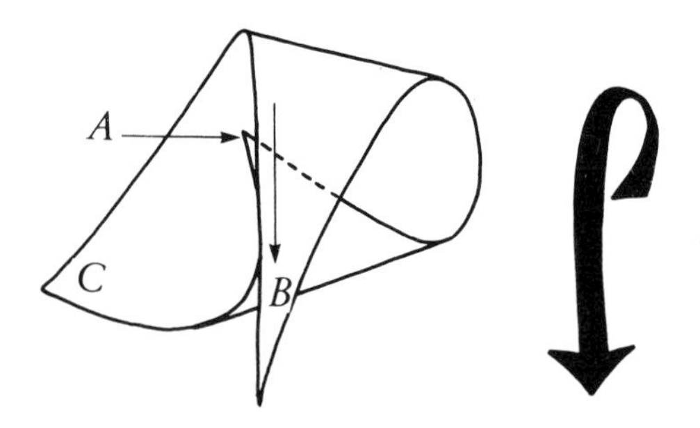

4 Gently pull point B, keeping the two edges as parallel as possible and ensuring the arrow B-C remains in line with the arrow A-C.

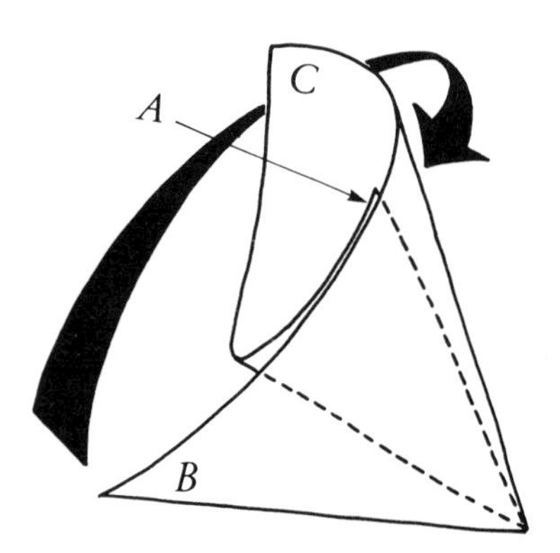

5 Continue until point A (now underneath) is within 18mm (3/4in) of the right angle C. Then take point B around the back of the cone and place under the thumb.

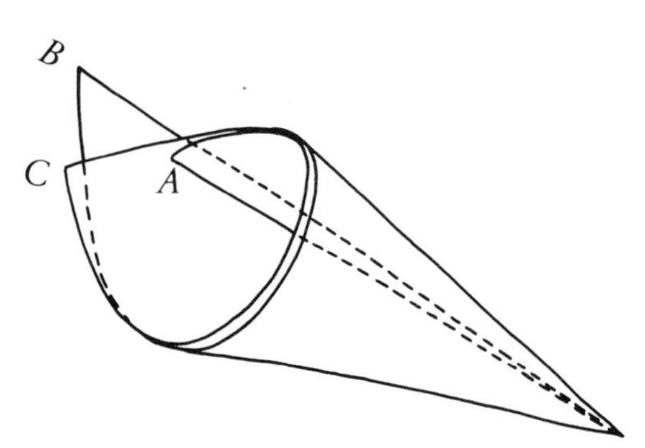

6 Point B is slightly to the right of point C – the three points do not meet. Make sure that the bag is tight and that there is no hole at the pointed end. If necessary, gently pull point A up slightly to tighten the cone.

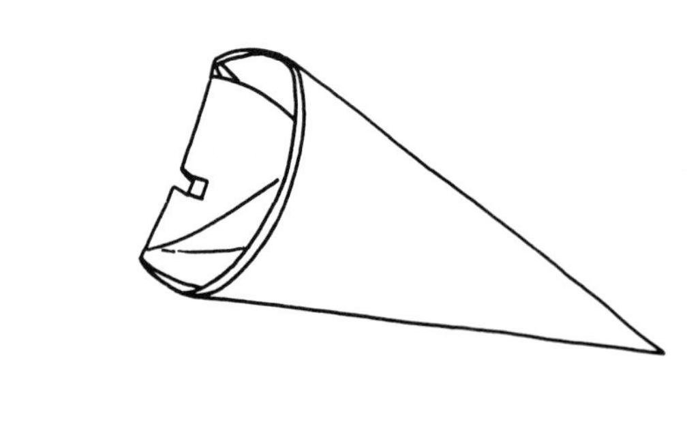

7 Fold all three points over and into the bag. Tear two small niches about 6mm (1/4in) apart and fold the resulting flap towards the inside of the bag, which is now ready for filling.

Basic Lettering

□BIRTHDAY BOY□

Ingredients
sponge cake baked in numeral tin (pan) or 20-cm (8-in) square cake tin
900g (2lb) sugarpaste
Cornish cream food colouring
dark brown food colouring
buttercream
boiled, sieved apricot jam (optional)
icing (confectioner's) sugar for dusting
250g (9oz) chocolate matchsticks
royal icing

Equipment
25 x 35-cm (10 x 14-in) cake board
rolling pin
palette knife
sharp knife
flexible plastic smoother
plastic wild animals
4 yellow candles
No1 nozzle
No6 nozzle
vegetable parchment piping bags

This is a good example of the type of cake that will appeal to a little boy. It has the minimum of decoration and relies on its bold chunky shape for impact. A sponge cake, baked in the shape of the number four, has been transformed into an enclosure for wild animals.

If possible, hire or buy a numeral cake frame as it is wasteful to cut the shape of the number four from a slab cake. If you make the cake in a numeral frame, bake it with the frame upside down, so that when the cake is turned out, the original base forms a flat top.

If you don't have a tin (pan) in the shape of a four, you can cut out the required shape from a 20-cm (8-in) square cake. Using a very sharp serrated knife, cut a large section from one corner, following the diagram. Cut a small triangular section from the centre of the sponge. Alternatively, divide the cake into three equal pieces. Use one piece to form the vertical bar, trim another and position at an angle of 45°, and divide the remaining piece for the 'foot' and 'tail', following the diagram.

The method of covering this cake with sugarpaste is slightly different from that usually followed, since it is quicker on this occasion to roll out the icing for the sides and top separately.

Colour the sugarpaste with Cornish cream food colouring. Roll two-thirds of the icing into a sausage, then flatten it with a rolling pin and roll out a strip equal in width to the depth of the cake, long enough to fit all round the sides and about 6mm (¼in) thick. If you can't manage to do this in one long strip, make sure the join is positioned so that it will not be seen from the front.

Spread a thin layer of buttercream or apricot jam over the surface of the cake. Then mould the strip of sugarpaste against the sides of the cake. Try to keep the corners sharply defined. Roll out the remaining sugarpaste and turn it over on to a dusting of sifted icing (confectioner's) sugar to prevent it sticking to the flat surface. Carefully turn the cake upside down and lay it on the sugarpaste. Use a sharp knife to cut the sugarpaste to fit the top of the cake, taking care to achieve a neat edge which will form a clean join between the sides and top. Carefully turn the cake the right way up and smooth the join with the palm of your hand to seal the edges. Use a flexible plastic smoother to 'polish' the sugarpaste.

Fill the triangular hole in the centre with chocolate matchsticks. To make the stockade, secure chocolate matchsticks with a little buttercream around the cake. Alternatively, chocolate finger biscuits (cookies) could be used. The wild animals are held in place with small dabs of buttercream.

Any leftover sugarpaste that is free from cake crumbs can be used to make a plaque inscribed with the little boy's name. Write his name on a piece of paper; then, using this as a template, scribe the outlines on to the sugarpaste and pipe over them in chocolate-coloured royal icing with a No1 nozzle. Leave to dry. Alternatively, use a brown food colouring pen. Pipe four stars with the chocolate-coloured royal icing and a No6 nozzle to hold the candles. Place the candles in position before the icing sets.

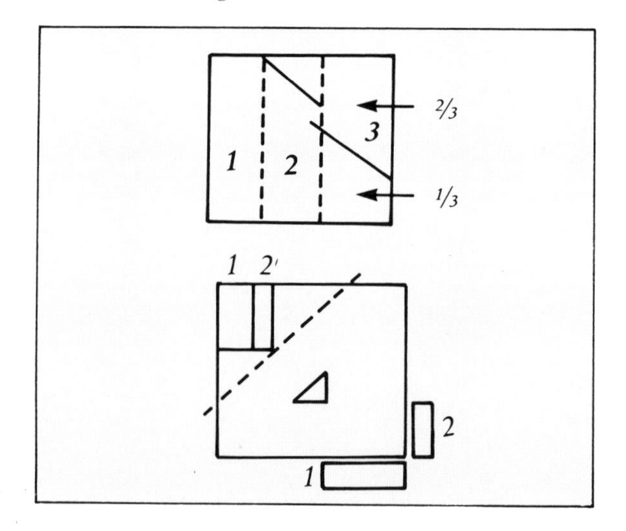

Stuart

WOODLAND SCENE

Ingredients
sponge cake baked in numeral tin (pan) or 20-cm (8-in) round cake and 15-cm (6-in) square cake tins
700g (1½lb) marzipan
1.4kg (3lb) sugarpaste
125g (4oz) royal icing
apple green food colouring
lemon yellow food colouring
rose pink food colouring
royal icing

Equipment
27.5-cm (11-in) square cake board
rolling pin
pastry brush
No1 or No2 crimper
No4 crimper
No1 nozzle
No2 nozzle
No4 nozzle
No37 forget-me-not nozzle
No66 leaf nozzle
vegetable parchment piping bags
3 yellow candles
3 wafer roses
24 edible sugar flowers
garlic press, reserved for cake decorating, or wire sieve
waxed paper
scriber or sharp-pointed needle

When planning a birthday cake for a very young child, a good rule to remember is that the simpler the design, the more effective the cake. Here, a sponge cake baked in the shape of the number three has been decorated with piped flowers, sugar rabbits and the name of the birthday girl herself.

Colour some sugarpaste apple green, then roll it out to the shape of the cake board. Brush the under-side of the paste with a little water before applying it to the board. Trim the edges by pressing the end of a No1 or No2 crimper through the sugarpaste to cut off the excess.

If you don't have a tin (pan) in the shape of a three, you can cut out the required shape from a 20-cm (8-in) round cake and a 15-cm (6-in) square cake. Cut the square cake in half, cut a wedge off one end of each half and position on the cake board, following the diagram. Cut a circle out of the centre of the round cake, then cut a wedge from one side to form a horseshoe and place at the base of the pieces you have already assembled. Alternatively, bake the second cake in a 22.5-cm (9-in) ring tin. Sandwich the pieces together with buttercream, or layers of jam and buttercream.

Cover the cake with a layer of marzipan, if the child likes it, and then a layer of sugarpaste *(see page 12)*. Decorate the top edge of the cake with a No4 crimper. Using green-coloured royal icing and a No1 nozzle, pipe blades of grass round the sides of the cake, then decorate the sides with edible sugar flowers, held in place with dots of royal icing. These flowers can be bought from specialist cake decorating shops or piped with a No37 nozzle. Place the three candles in the small wafer roses, which are also available from specialist shops, and pipe on leaves with green-coloured royal icing and a No66 leaf nozzle. To make the small bushes to the right and left of the cake, roll some green-coloured sugarpaste into a ball, then place it in a garlic press and squeeze it through the holes to make a dense mass of green strands. The sugarpaste can also be pushed through a wire sieve to achieve the same effect. Fix the strands to the sugarpaste-covered cake board with a little water, and add a few edible sugar flowers for colour.

The rabbits can be bought from specialist cake decorating shops or piped with royal icing. Using a No4 nozzle and brown-coloured or white royal icing, pipe a large teardrop, about 2.5cm (1in) long and

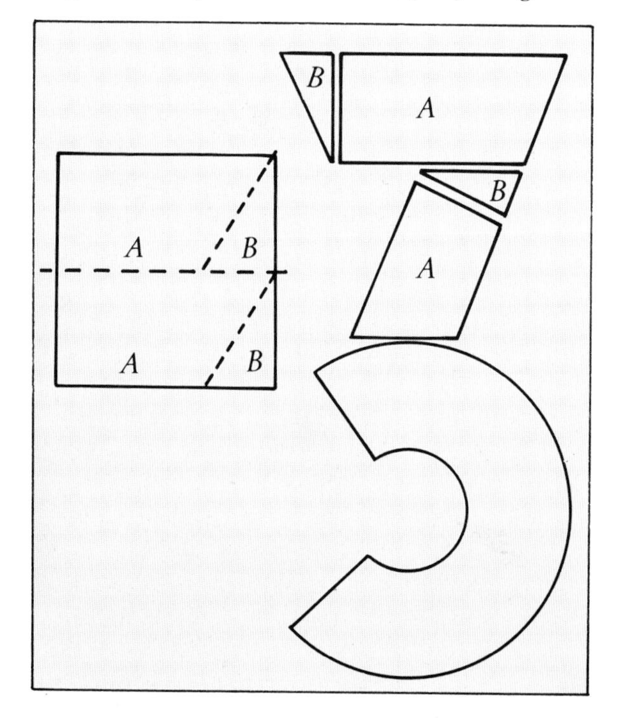

12mm (½in) wide at the largest end, on to waxed paper. At the pointed end of the teardrop, pipe two small balls of icing to represent the front paws and, at the wide end of the teardrop, pipe a small ball for the tail. To make the ears, pipe two long teardrops towards the head, then overpipe around the edge of each one with a No2 nozzle to emphasise the shape of the ear and leave to dry. When the icing is hard, pipe in two small dots for the eyes, a dot for the nose and another for the mouth. You can use food colouring pens if you prefer. Gently peel the paper from the rabbits and position them on the cake board.

Write a message, such as the child's name, on a piece of paper, then, using this as a template, follow the outlines with a scriber or sharp-pointed needle on to the sugarpaste, and pipe over them with a No1 nozzle. Leave to dry.

COMING OF AGE

Ingredients

fruit cakes baked in numeral tins (pans) or 20-cm (8-in) square, 17.5-cm (7-in) and 15-cm (6-in) round tins
boiled, sieved apricot jam or egg white
1.6kg (3½lb) marzipan
sherry or other alcohol
2.6kg (5lb) sugarpaste
royal icing
lemon yellow food colouring

Equipment

30 x 45-cm (12 x 18-in) rectangular cake board
5-cm (2-in) stainless steel biscuit (cookie) cutter
sharp knife
rolling pin
pastry brush
No4 crimper
No24 fluting crimper
flexible plastic smoother
palette knife
2 metres (2 yards) yellow satin ribbon, 3-mm (⅛-in) wide
vegetable parchment piping bags
No1 nozzle
No2 nozzle
No42 nozzle
scriber or sharp-pointed needle

An eighteenth birthday tends to be celebrated more now than a twenty-first. It may even be the last time that the guest of honour wants his or her age made public by the design of the cake! If you do not have access to numeral-shaped tins (pans) or frames, it is not difficult to make the numbers required for this cake by cutting them from slab cakes. Whether these are fruit-based or sponge, they must be left overnight before cutting, in order to minimise crumbing. Turn them upside down, so that the smooth bases become the tops.

Cut the number 'one' from a 20-cm (8-in) square cake, following the diagram. Cut the 'eight' from a 15-cm (6-in) and a 17.5-cm (7-in) round cake, following the diagram. Use a stainless steel biscuit (cookie) cutter to make a 5-cm (2-in) diameter hole in the centre of both round cakes, then cut a 2.5-cm (1-in) slice from each cake – this is where the two rings will be stuck together.

Brush the cakes with apricot jam or egg white, then cover with a layer of marzipan. Moisten the marzipan with a little sherry or other alcohol to sterilise the surface and to make it sticky enough to attach the sugarpaste *(see page 12)*.

If you prefer to use sponge cakes, they may be coated with sugarpaste without an initial layer of marzipan. Stick the parts of the cake together with jam, or jam and buttercream. Then spread a thin layer of buttercream over the entire surface and put the cakes in the fridge for about 1 hour before applying the sugarpaste. This firms the buttercream, making it easier to apply the coating of sugarpaste.

Roll out some sugarpaste to the shape of the cake board. Brush the under-side of the paste with a little water before applying it to the board. Use a No4 crimper to make two parallel lines all round the edges of the board.

Each cake is covered with a single piece of sugarpaste. It is helpful to roll this out to a rectangular shape. As both cakes are about 30 x 15 cm (12 x 6 in) at their longest and widest points, the sugarpaste should be about 45 x 30 cm (18 x 12 in). The icing will stretch and accept a great deal of easing and moulding as you shape it to the contours of the cakes. Use a flexible plastic smoother and the natural warmth of your hands to seal any cracks and to help to adjust the sugarpaste to the shapes.

Coat the insides of the two centres in the 'eight' with sugarpaste before covering the rest of the cake. To do this, cut a strip three times the width of the hole, roll it up like a bandage and drop it into the centre. Unwind it with your fingers, making sure that the join is towards the front, so that it cannot be seen when you are looking at the cake from that side. Use your fingers to push the sugarpaste against the sides and make it level with the top of the cake.

After covering the 'eight' with sugarpaste and smoothing it over, you will see the two indentations caused by the central holes. In the middle of each, cut a small cross, then very carefully cut away the excess sugarpaste until you can join the top icing to the previously coated area. Use your hands to smooth and seal the two together.

After both cakes are covered, add the decoration on the sides. Use a No24 crimper, held vertically, and bring the side of the cake right to the edge of the flat surface. By doing this, you can take the edge of the crimper to the lower part of the cakes. Crimp right round each to form a textured pattern on the bottom third of the icing. With a No4 crimper, add two parallel lines of crimping, allowing enough room between them for 3-mm (⅛-in) wide ribbon to be attached. With the same

No4 crimper, form two parallel lines on the top surface of each cake.

With a broad palette knife or large plastic smoother, lift one of the cakes, hold it in position just above the prepared cake board, let the top end of the cake just touch the surface of the board, then quickly withdraw the knife or smoother. The cake will drop into place, needing very little further adjustment.

Pipe a small dot of royal icing on the back of the ribbon and, starting at the back of the cake, pin it in place between the two parallel lines of crimping. Proceed round the cake, piping a small dot of icing at 7.5-cm (3-in) intervals and then pinning the ribbon in position. When the icing is dry, remove the pins by placing a finger lightly on each side of the pin and twisting it gently before withdrawing it. Using a No42 nozzle pipe a shell border around the base of the cake. Put the ribbon on the second cake before positioning it on the board and piping the shell border.

Use a No2 nozzle to pipe yellow-coloured royal icing for the thicker lines between the two parallel lines of crimping, then overpipe using a No1 nozzle for the thinner lines. Make a template of the words 'Happy Birthday' and scratch the greeting on to the top of the cake with a scriber or sharp-pointed needle. Pipe over the outlines with a No1 nozzle.

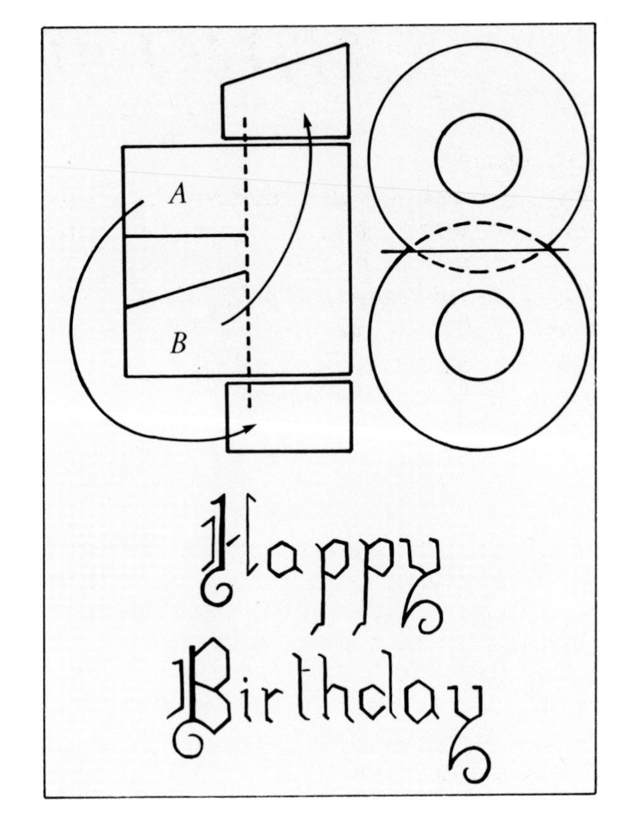

□CHICO THE CLOWN□

Ingredients
2.2kg (4½lb) fruit cake mixture
700g (1½lb) marzipan
1.1kg (2½lb) sugarpaste
boiled, sieved apricot jam or egg white
water or alcohol
50g (2oz) petal paste or pastillage
cornflower blue food colouring
moss green food colouring
red food colouring
skintone food colouring

Equipment
large spherical tin (pan)
pastry brush
baking sheet
rolling pin
sharp knife
27.5-cm (11-in) round cake board
No2 crimper
No9 crimper
piece of plastic or polythene
wooden skewer or paintbrush
palette knife
ridged marzipan modelling tool or large fork
round-ended modelling tool
silver plastic wedding ring decoration
cotton wool balls
3 red sugar flowers

This cake is baked in a spherical tin (pan) used for cooking traditional Christmas puddings. Brush the two halves of the tin with melted fat and sprinkle them with flour, or spray with a special non-stick aerosol, then completely fill one half with mixture but only half-fill the other. Clamp the two halves together, then secure them in a simple stand to prevent them moving. A hole in the upper half of the tin lets the moisture escape, as the cake mixture expands to fill the void. Turn the cake out while it is still hot and leave it to cool on a baking sheet – a wire rack would leave indentations in the base.

Roll out the marzipan, then cut out a 10-cm (4-in) diameter circle. When you pick up the cake you will see it has developed a flat area where it has rested while cooling, so apply the disc of marzipan to that part, having first brushed it with the apricot jam or egg white. Brush the cake with the jam or egg white, then drape the marzipan over the cake, encouraging it to fit the sides snugly by moulding it with the palms of your hands and compressing it where it meets the circle of marzipan. Do not let it form any folds or pleats. Trim any excess marzipan from the join around the base, then put the cake aside for 24 hours to allow the marzipan to harden. Colour some sugarpaste with skintone food colouring, then apply it to the cake in the same way.

Decorate the cake board with a thin layer of blue-coloured sugarpaste and trim the edge with a No9 crimper. To make the ruffles, knead together equal quantities of petal paste and sugarpaste. The resulting mixture is slightly stiffer than sugarpaste and can be rolled very thinly, although it is more brittle when dry. Colour half the paste light blue and leave the rest white. Roll out both pastes, then cut out a 22.5-cm (9-in) diameter circle from the blue-coloured paste and a slightly smaller one from the white paste. Cover the white circle with a piece of plastic or polythene while you are working on the other one, to prevent it drying out. Roll a wooden skewer, or the smooth round handle of a paintbrush, around the edge of the circle, simultaneously pressing it into the paste to make it stretch slightly and pucker, so as to give a fluted and frilled effect. When you have worked all the way round the circle, pick it up with a palette knife and place it in the middle of the cake board, securing it by moistening the centre with water. Repeat the procedure with the white circle and place it on top of the blue one.

The clown's head is decorated entirely with coloured sugarpaste. Begin with the ears, colouring some sugarpaste in a slightly deeper tone than that used for the head. Mould it into two sausages, about 7.5cm (3in) long and 12mm (½in) thick. Working on one ear at a time, dampen one side and push it into position, shaping it like a question mark. Smooth it into place with a round-ended modelling tool or the rounded end of a bone-handled knife. Place a silver plastic wedding ring from a specialist cake decorator's shop into the lobe of one ear to give the clown more character.

Begin the face by cutting out the mouth from white sugarpaste, using a template made from the pattern provided *(see page 68)*. Carefully cut out the centre of the mouth and use this white sugarpaste as a template to cut out the lips from a piece of thinly rolled red-coloured sugarpaste. Place the red lips in the middle of the white mouth and smooth over them gently with a rolling pin to close any gaps and mould the pieces together. Turn the icing over and moisten the back with a little water, then carefully lift it and position it on the cake.

The blue and white parts of the eyes are prepared and secured in position in the same way, then cut out two thin strips of red-coloured sugarpaste and stick these over the eyes. To make the nose, mould a ball of red-coloured sugarpaste and form it into a cone, the pointed end of which is pushed into a depression made in the cake just above the mouth.

Make the hair from short strips of thinly rolled petal paste that has been deeply scored with a ridged marzipan modelling tool, or the back of an ordinary dinner fork. Stick it to the head with a little water, supporting the curls with small balls of cotton wool until they have set hard.

To make the hat, roll out a thick cylinder of sugarpaste and flare it out at one end to form the rim. Decorate around it with a No2 crimper to create a scalloped effect. Add a thin circle of sugarpaste to the battered and worn crown of the hat to look like a lid that is prevented from closing by a few bright red sugar flowers growing inside. Carefully place the head in the centre of the frills, securing it in place with a little water or alcohol.

CINDERELLA'S PUMPKIN COACH

Ingredients
2.2kg (4½lb) fruit cake mixture
700g (1½lb) marzipan
1.1kg (2½lb) sugarpaste
boiled, sieved apricot jam or egg white
water or alcohol
225g (8oz) caster (superfine) sugar
5ml (1 tsp) egg white
apple green food colouring
black food colouring
dark brown food colouring
peach food colouring
pink food colouring (optional)
red food colouring
fuchsia pink dusting powder
skintone dusting powder
150g (5oz) petal paste
150g (5oz) marzipan or sugarpaste for frog
125g (4oz) royal icing
piping gel

Equipment
large spherical tin (pan)
15-cm (6-in) round cake card and 30 x 45-cm (12 x 18-in) rectangular cake board
7.5-cm (3-in) round wooden block (optional)
ruler or plastic smoother
crescent-shaped embossing tool
mouse-shaped moulds
2 sheets of rice paper
black food colouring pen
blue food colouring pen
brown food colouring pen
candy pink food colouring pen
green food colouring pen
tangerine food colouring pen
sharp knife
dogbone modelling tool
cone-shaped modelling tool or wooden skewer
rolling pin
round pastry cutters
4 wooden skewers or pieces of dowel
No5 nozzle
vegetable parchment piping bag
2 metres (2 yards) peach satin ribbon, 3-mm (⅛-in) wide
sugar flowers or other decorations

Bake the fruit cake mixture in a large spherical tin (pan) used for cooking traditional Christmas puddings. Turn it out while it is still warm *(see page 22)* and leave to cool on a baking sheet. Then cover the cake with marzipan and peach-coloured sugarpaste *(see page 22)*, but do not cut out a circular piece of sugarpaste for the base. Stand the cake on a 15-cm (6-in) round cake card or, if you wish to create the impression that the coach is clear of the ground and supported by its wheels, place a small 7.5-cm (3-in) round wooden block beneath the centre of the cake card. Before the sugarpaste covering on the cake has time to harden, mark it into sections, using the edge of a ruler or a large plastic smoother, and use a crescent-shaped embossing tool to decorate the doors of the pumpkin coach with a quilted texture. Set the cake to one side and leave the sugarpaste to harden.

To make the sugar mice, mix the caster (superfine) sugar with the egg white. The sugar should have the texture of wet sand, so

if it feels too dry, add a little more egg white, and add a little more sugar if it is too wet. If you wish, you can colour the mice by stirring in a little pink food colouring to the sugar mixture, ensuring that the colour is completely dispersed. Pack the mixture into the moulds as firmly as possible, then turn out immediately and leave to dry overnight.

To make the carriage wheels, roll out the white petal paste until it is about 3mm (⅛in) thick, then make templates of the wheels and coachman's seat from the patterns provided *(see pages 26-27)* and cut them out of the paste. You will need two large wheels, two small ones and one seat. Leave the pieces to dry for 24 hours.

For the carriage windows, cut out two identically-shaped pieces of rice paper using the template for the side windows, then on one window draw in the outline of Cinderella using a brown food colouring pen for the head and arm, and a candy pink pen for the dress. Colour in the figure with skintone and fuchsia pink dusting powders. Draw the details on the other window in reverse, by turning the pattern over – otherwise the design will not be facing forwards when viewed from either side. Cut out the front window using the template provided, but leave undecorated.

To make the frog coachman, colour most of the marzipan or sugarpaste green, then take a piece the size of a walnut and form it into a cone or pear shape to make the body of the frog. To make the legs, roll out a sausage-shaped piece of green-coloured sugarpaste about 6.25cm (2½in) long and 12mm (½in) thick. Using a dogbone modelling tool, or your little finger, indent the sausage in two places to form the knee and ankle joints, then cut the sausage in half lengthways with a sharp knife. Lift up one piece and, taking the smaller end, flatten it between your finger and thumb to broaden it and form the foot, then mark this into three with a knife to give the impression of a webbed foot. Do the same to the other leg. Attach the legs to the cone and drape one over the other to cross them. Make the jacket from a small piece of red-coloured sugarpaste, rolling it out until it is very thin, then cut out a 5-cm (2-in) diameter circle. Using a smaller round cutter, cut out a crescent shape from one edge of the circle to

form the neck. Wrap the circle of sugarpaste around the cone, turning out the ends of the crescent to form the collar. To make the arms, roll out a thin sausage of red-coloured sugarpaste about 10cm (4in) long, leaving the ends slightly thicker than the middle. Indent the ends to form the cuffs with a cone-shaped modelling tool or the pointed end of a wooden skewer. Drape this piece around the back of the cone to form the arms. Make the hands by taking a piece of green-coloured sugarpaste about the size of a hazelnut, cutting it in half and forming two cones. Flatten the broader end between your finger and thumb, then, using a sharp knife, mark these into three to form the webbed fingers. Dampen the pointed ends and push them into the cuffs. To make the head, take a piece of green-coloured sugarpaste about the size of a hazelnut and roll it into a very fat pear shape. Cut along the thinner edge of the pear and open it out to form the mouth. Roll two small pea-sized balls of green-coloured sugarpaste for the eyes. Use the pointed end of a modelling tool or wooden skewer to attach each eye to the head, and fill the resulting hollow area with white royal icing and leave to dry, then mark the eye balls with a black food colouring pen. Attach the head to the body with a little water or royal icing and leave to dry.

To decorate the cake board, stick two or three lumps of marzipan or sugarpaste to the board, then cover them with a thin layer of green-coloured sugarpaste. Mix together any coloured scraps of marzipan you have left with any remaining plain marzipan, colour it grey or brown, then roll out to create a marbled effect for the road. Place this on top of the sugarpaste. Place the cake in position.

Stick the windows on to the sides and front of the cake with piping gel, then pipe in the details of the door frames and windows with a No5 nozzle and white royal icing. Cut out a piece of green-coloured sugarpaste to make the calyx and stem of the pumpkin and stick it on top of the cake. Stick the coachman's seat in position and leave to dry. Mark the spokes of the wheels with a brown food colouring pen and secure them to the cake with wooden skewers or pieces of dowel. Position the mice, pipe in their tails and eyes and harness them together with the ribbon. Place the frog on the seat and put all the ribboned reins in his webbed fingers. To finish the cake, add sugar flowers or similar decorations along the roadside. These are available from specialist cake decorating shops.

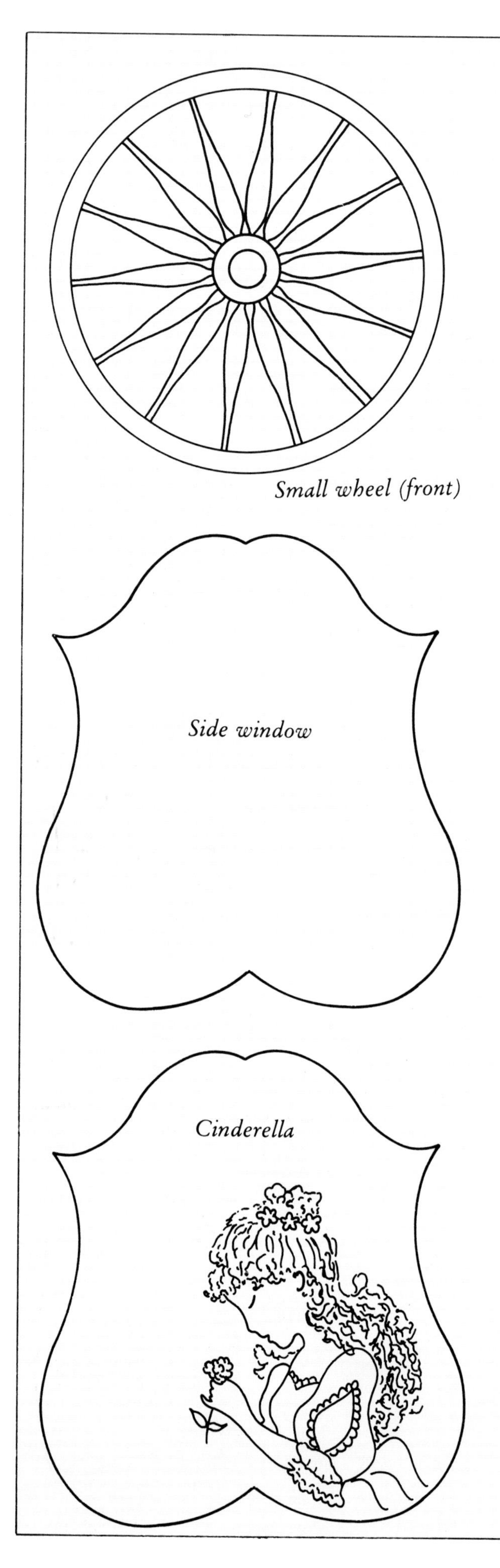

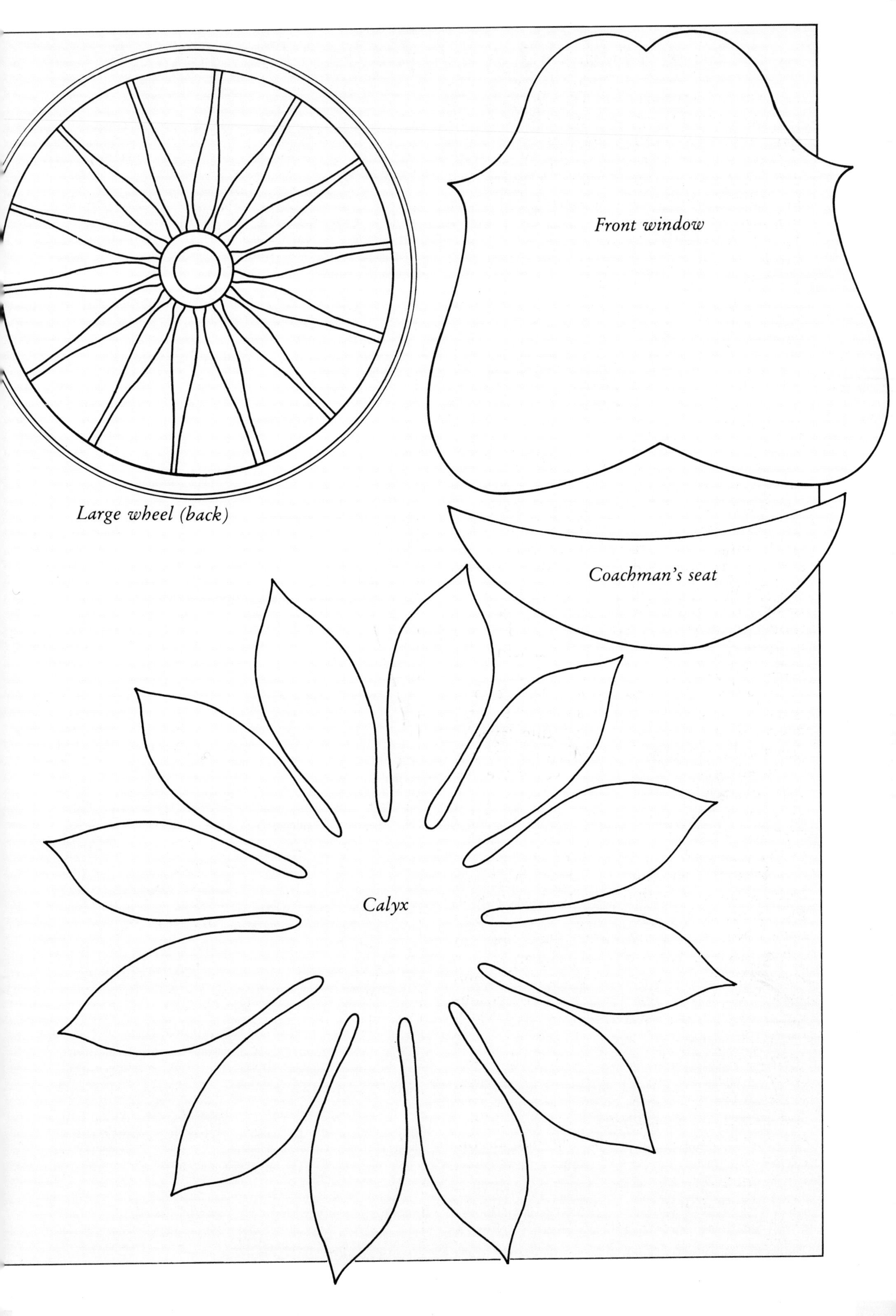
Large wheel (back)
Front window
Coachman's seat
Calyx

□PARISIAN POODLES□

Ingredients
fruit cake baked in 20-cm (8-in) round cake tin (pan)
1.1kg (2½lb) sugarpaste
boiled, sieved apricot jam or egg white
700g (1½lb) marzipan
sherry or other alcohol
black food colouring
red food colouring
rose pink food colouring
225g (8oz) royal icing

Equipment
32.5-cm (13-in) round cake board
rolling pin
No6 crimper
tracing paper
scriber or sharp-pointed needle
vegetable parchment piping bags
No0 nozzle
No1 nozzle
No4 nozzle
No7 nozzle
black food colouring pen

This cake was originally created for a young lady who was given a surprise weekend in Paris as a birthday present. The design captures the city's atmosphere with its pavement cafés and the Eiffel Tower. When you have learned the simple rules of pressure piping, you will find that the most imaginatively decorated cakes can be completed with surprising speed. It takes no more than 5 minutes to finish the sketch which is repeated around the side of the cake, while each poodle can be piped in about 90 seconds.

The fundamental principle of pressure piping is that simple figures are always more effective than anatomically precise ones. Provided that they are easily identified and are amusing to look at when their most prominent features are emphasised, they are likely to be successful. To help to establish the proportions of objects to be piped in half relief against the sides or top of a cake, think of them as matchstick figures and, if necessary, mark their outline on the surface with a scriber.

Cover the board with a 6mm (¼in) thick layer of pink-coloured sugarpaste and crimp round the edge with a No6 crimper.

Cover the cake with marzipan and then pink-coloured sugarpaste *(see page 12)*. Use a small cone of moistened sugarpaste to stick the cake to the centre of the board. Pipe a shell border in a deeper pink-coloured royal icing around the base of the cake with a No7 nozzle.

Trace the drawing of the street scene and using this as a template, scratch the design on to the side of the cake with a scriber or sharp-pointed needle. Repeat twice more, leaving equal space between each sketch. Fill in the major outlines with a black food colouring pen. If time is not at a premium, you could use the brush embroidery technique *(see page 30)* to give depth to the awning over the café door and to the table tops, and to embellish the wrought iron of the lamp-post and the Eiffel Tower in the background.

Then make the three poodles sitting round the side of the cake, following the diagrams *(see page 69)*. Starting at the base of the cake next to the shell border, pipe the body with white royal icing and a No4 nozzle. Decrease the amount of pressure as the nozzle moves up the side of the cake so that the body tapers towards the head. Then pipe the hind leg, starting at the haunch. Tuck the end of the nozzle into the base of the body, increasing the pressure as the nozzle moves in a reverse C back to where it started. Then pipe from the base of the body to form the lower part of the leg, finishing with a slight increase in pressure to form the paw. Pipe two front paws, starting from the shoulder and moving down towards the base of the cake, decreasing the pressure slightly at the base for the ankle and then increasing again slightly for the paws. Make the head by piping a large teardrop of icing just above where the neck has tapered, then increasing the pressure to form the front of the head. Pipe the ears. Leave the icing to dry slightly, while piping the other poodles. Then using a No0 nozzle, pipe the curly hair on the feet, hindquarters, shoulders, tail tip, topknot, ears and paws. The easiest way to do this is to hold the tip of the nozzle about 12mm (½in) away from the point to be decorated and squeeze the bag as hard as possible. As the icing is expelled, it will form curls and twists of its own accord. Pipe the details of the eyes, nose and mouth with a No0 nozzle, or draw them using food colouring pens. If liked, you can give each poodle a drinking bowl and a bone.

To make the poodle for the top of the cake, use the No4 nozzle to pipe the body, starting with a large ball or dome of icing for the hindquarters. Hold the bag vertically and squeeze out a large ball. Keeping the tip of the nozzle in the icing and the pressure constant, bring the nozzle forwards and downwards so that the icing tapers to form the front part of the body. Pipe the two front legs, crossing them about 5cm (2in) from the paws and finish by increasing the pressure slightly to form the front paws. The hind legs are piped in the same way as those on the side of the cake. Start at the base and with quite a lot of pressure, bring the nozzle up to the top of the body, then down to where the leg begins and out at an angle to form the lower part, again finishing with an increase of pressure for the paw. Pipe the tail from the base of the hindquarters and bring it up over the back of the poodle. Build up a short sausage of icing at the tapered end of the body for the neck. Place the nozzle three-quarters of the way up and pipe horizontally from the front of the sausage to form the front of the head. Pipe the ears, and whiskers at the end of the muzzle. Leave the icing to dry slightly, then add the curly hair as described above.

Finish the cake by piping the greeting with white royal icing and a No1 nozzle.

ORCHID CAKE

Ingredients
fruit cake baked in 20-cm (8-in) hexagonal cake tin (pan)
boiled, sieved apricot jam or egg white
900g (2lb) marzipan
sherry or other alcohol
900g (2lb) sugarpaste
apple green food colouring
2.5ml (½ tsp) piping gel
225g (8oz) royal icing, preferably made the previous day

Equipment
25-cm (10-in) hexagonal cake board
pastry brush
rolling pin
tilting turntable or wedge
tracing paper
scriber or sharp-pointed needle
vegetable parchment piping bags
No0 nozzle No1 nozzle No5 nozzle
No3 sable paintbrush

Not every birthday cake has to be decorated with an extravagant or witty design – sometimes an elegantly understated approach is more appropriate. This brush embroidery technique is used on a cake which has been covered with very pale green-coloured sugarpaste. The object is to create an effect similar to heavily embroidered lace. It is achieved by piping the outline of the pattern and then dispersing the icing with a very soft sable paintbrush. The addition of a little piping gel to the icing gives it a smooth and creamy consistency.

Cover the cake with marzipan. Colour the sugarpaste a very pale green and cover the cake *(see page 12)*. Position it on the board and allow the icing to harden for at least 48 hours before decorating.

Trace the designs provided *(see page 70)* and use these as templates. Transfer them to the cake by scratching through the pattern on to the surface of the icing with a scriber or sharp-pointed needle. It may be necessary to trace the patterns more than once, since the paper may be extensively cut during the scribing process. Do not use lead pencil to trace directly on to the cake. The amount of graphite involved is minimal but it is not recommended as a food additive!

Although the icing will remain in position as it is brushed into place, it is convenient to work on a surface that is as nearly horizontal as possible. Therefore use either a tilting turntable to slant the cake at the correct angle or wedge the board with a block at the front. The next best alternative is to position the cake so that when brushing out the pattern on the sides, the design is at eye level approximately.

Add the piping gel to the royal icing. Begin by piping round the outline of the features in the background with a No1 nozzle. Pipe a second line of icing close to the first, just inside the edge of each leaf or petal. Begin brushing immediately using a No3 sable paintbrush. This should be moistened with water and gently squeezed between the fingers to flatten the hairs together and to give them a slight surve. Stroke the still-soft icing from the outside of the piped lines towards the centre or base of the design, using the curved side of the brush, not just its tip. Regular gentle strokes will result in a smooth even finish. You will achieve a more realistic result on the leaves and petals if the direction of the brush strokes follows the general direction of their veins and other natural contours. The veins themselves may be piped with a No0 nozzle while the brush work is still wet, in which case they will blend into the background icing. If a raised result is required, they can be piped when the brushed icing is dry. Plan the order in which the design is completed so that the foreground features are the last to be finished.

When the design is finished, its entire surface will have a coating of icing. Greater realism can be attained if the icing is graduated in thickness to achieve a raised effect along the outline and at points of interest towards the centre. Further contrast may be obtained by piping a second heavy line of icing on to the foreground of the design when it has dried. The additional icing must then be very carefully brushed out at the edges to form a continuous smooth join with the rest of the design.

Using a No1 nozzle, pipe and brush the individual pieces of fern first. Then pipe all three back petals of each orchid, the centre curved back petal having quite a heavy edge. Pipe and brush the wide frilled petal on each side of the orchid tongue. Then pipe the large frilled tongue and finally pipe and brush the bell shape above the tongue. All the veins on the petals should be piped with a No0 nozzle before they dry so that they will soften and merge into the brushed icing.

Pipe a shell border around the base of the cake with a No5 nozzle and royal icing.

□CARPENTER'S CAKE□

Ingredients
sponge cake baked in 30-cm (12-in) square cake tin (pan)
jam
buttercream
900g (2lb) sugarpaste
black food colouring
chestnut food colouring
dark brown food colouring
silver food colouring
skintone food colouring
100g (3½oz) petal paste

Equipment
45-cm (18-in) oval cake board
palette knife
sharp serrated knife
cocktail stick (wooden toothpick)
rolling pin
20-cm (8-in) wooden dowel
45-cm (18-in) beige acetate ribbon, 3-mm (⅛-in) wide

If the man in your life still hasn't finished the kitchen cupboards he promised to make a year ago, maybe you should give him a carpenter's plane as a hint on his birthday.

Cut the sponge cake into thirds to make rectangles about 30 x 10cm (12 x 4in) and lay them on top of one another with a filling of jam and buttercream between the layers. Alternatively, if you have a multi-size tin (pan), move the partition to the 10-cm (4-in) slot and bake the cake 7.5-cm (3-in) deep. Cut out a shallow rectangular section from the top of the cake, following the diagram *(see page 71)*, and then spread the entire surface with a thin layer of buttercream. Put the cake in the fridge and leave for 1 hour to harden.

Colour the sugarpaste a very pale brown. Then use a cocktail stick (wooden toothpick) to wipe the ball of sugarpaste with some more dark brown, some chestnut and a little black food colouring. Knead the sugarpaste once or twice, working it in one direction only. Roll it out and you will see that the sugarpaste has a marbled or woodgrain effect where the colourings have not mixed evenly.

Cover the cake with the sugarpaste *(see page 12)*, being careful to press it down into the shallow depression cut in the top. Trim the sugarpaste especially carefully along the base, as there is no shell border on this cake to hide any flaws.

To make the handle for the front of the plane, roll a ball of the sugarpaste between the palms of your hands and stick it in place with a little water. Colour a little sugarpaste with dark brown food colouring and use to make a small disc. Place this on top of the handle and add a tiny circle of white sugarpaste marked in the centre to represent the head of the screw securing it. Mould some marbled sugarpaste over a wooden dowel to make the handgrip for the back of the plane, and push the end into the cake at an angle. Make the top of the handgrip by rolling out a piece of the darker brown sugarpaste thinly and cutting it into a teardrop shape. Add a small circle of white sugarpaste marked in the centre to represent the screw-head. To make the blade, trace the template provided, lay this on a piece of thinly rolled petal paste and cut round with a sharp knife. Leave to dry, then paint the blade with silver food colouring, leaving the central area white.

The need to add extra details relating to the mechanism for adjusting the blade of a real plane is avoided by filling the depression with 'woodshavings'. Those in the illustration have been made from short pieces of acetate ribbon curled by drawing them sharply along the back of a knife.

Use any remaining petal paste to make a gift tag to hang over the front of the plane. Write your greeting with a brown food colouring pen.

Happy
Birthday
Dad

SMILE PLEASE

Ingredients
chocolate sponge cake baked in 20-cm (8-in) round cake tin (pan)
vanilla sponge cake baked in 20-cm (8-in) round cake tin (pan)
buttercream
900g (2lb) plain (dark) chocolate
100g (3½oz) petal paste
icing (confectioner's) sugar
black food colouring
chestnut food colouring

Equipment
25-cm (10-in) round cake board
large round pastry cutter or cup and saucer
sharp serrated knife
palette knife
double boiler
wire cooling rack
baking tin (pan)
wire sieve
rolling pin
sharp knife
sable paintbrush
2 metres (2 yards) decorette ribbon
vegetable parchment piping bag

If your favourite man is unlikely to be moved by the beauty of cascading sugar flowers, choose one of his hobbies as the theme of the decoration for his birthday cake. One of the most popular themes is photography.

There are many brands of baker's (compound) chocolate, including chocolate-flavoured buttons, which are suitable to use for covering cakes. They do not require the same care in melting as eating chocolate or the couverture used by professional confectioners. Baker's chocolate is also cheaper, but it does not have the same distinctive flavour as true chocolate.

The contrasting colours of the two sponges can be used to make the cake more interesting when it is cut. If you do not have any large round cutters, use a cup and saucer as a guide and cut two circles, one smaller than the other, out of each sponge. Use a sharp serrated knife to cut vertically through the sponges. Separate the circles and reassemble reversing the colours. Sandwich the two sponges together with a little buttercream, taking care that the contrasting circles are not directly above each other. Seal the surface with a thin layer of buttercream spread over the top and sides with a palette knife. Leave in the fridge for about 1 hour for the buttercream to harden.

To cover the cake, break up the plain (dark) chocolate into 2.5-cm (1-in) cubes and melt it in the top of a double boiler or a bowl set over a pan of hot water. Do not try to save time by using boiling water in the outer pan. Water from the hot tap will give sufficient heat to melt the chocolate. It is very easy to spoil chocolate by overheating and once this happens, it never recovers its appearance or quality. If you cannot hold your finger in the water for 20 seconds, it is too hot. Be very careful not to splash even a single drop of water into the chocolate since, if you do, you will be unable to pour it smoothly and it will set with a dull or streaky finish.

Place the buttercream-covered cake on a wire rack over a baking tin (pan). Pour the melted chocolate through a wire sieve in a steady stream on to the centre of the cake. Using a wire sieve prevents any partially melted lumps from reaching the cake and disperses any air bubbles, thus helping to form a more even coating. Make sure that you have enough melted chocolate to allow it to flow down the sides of the cakes as well. If you are unable to make it flow evenly over all the surface, use a warmed palette knife to help to spread it while you pour. The chocolate sets very quickly so do not waste any time.

Make templates *(see page 72)* of the photographer and the wedges used to support the figure, and a small plaque for the inscription. Roll out the petal paste on a flat surface lightly dusted with icing (confectioner's) sugar. Lay the templates on top and cut round neatly with a sharp knife. Leave to dry on a wire rack for 24 hours. Using a sable paintbrush, paint the photographer's hood and shoes with black food colouring, and the camera, table, wedges and photographer's legs with chestnut food colouring. Pipe scrolls around the edge of the plaque using melted chocolate in a piping bag, then pipe the inscription. Stick the pieces in position with a little melted chocolate.

Alternatively, you can reproduce the design directly on a small plaque of petal paste which is then laid flat on top of the cake. Use a black food colouring pen to paint the photographer's hood and shoes, and a chestnut food colouring pen for the remaining features.

Finish the cake by tying decorette ribbon around its top and bottom. Pipe scrolls around the edge of the top of the cake with melted chocolate.

Dad

☐GIFT-WRAPPED☐

Ingredients
fruit cake baked in 12.5-cm (5-in) square cake tin (pan)
boiled, sieved apricot jam or egg white
600g (1¼lb) marzipan
sherry or other alcohol
600g (1¼lb) sugarpaste
royal icing

Equipment
20-cm (8-in) square cake board
rolling pin
embossing tool
large-headed pins
5 metres (5 yards) dark blue satin ribbon, 12-mm (½-in) wide
5 metres (5 yards) pale blue satin ribbon, 12-mm (½-in) wide
No42 nozzle
vegetable parchment piping bag
28-gauge white cotton-covered florists' wire
tweezers

A parcel cake is a very simple solution to the problem of choosing a design for a birthday cake, as it is one of the quickest of all cakes to decorate.

Cover the cake with marzipan and sugarpaste *(see page 12)*. Try to make the corners and sides of the cake as square as possible since this will add a little realism to the overall effect. While the sugarpaste is still soft, mark the sides and top with a special embossing tool. If you do not have one of these, you can use the ornamented end of a teaspoon or a moulded button – in fact, anything that has a raised pattern on it.

Using a large-headed pin, attach the end of the dark blue ribbon to the centre of one side of the cake at its base. Fit the ribbon snugly over the cake and cut it at the base on the other side, securing the end with a pin. Then fit more dark blue ribbon across the cake in the other direction. Repeat the process with the pale blue ribbon. Then pass one end of the pale blue ribbon underneath one of the ribbons already in position and weave it through those on the remaining three sides to fit round the cake horizontally. Cut it to the right length and pin it in place. Stick the ends to the side of the cake with a small dot of royal icing. Repeat the process with the dark blue ribbon. Remove the pins. Then carefully pull all the vertical ribbons taut and temporarily pin in position just above where the shell border will be piped.

Pipe a line of shells around the base of the parcel in white royal icing with a No42 nozzle, making sure that you cover the ends of the vertical ribbons beneath the shells. Remove the pins.

The large pompom bow on the top of the cake is made with about 15 pale and 15 dark blue ribbon loops and tails. Start by making three 5-cm (2-in) loops at one end of the ribbon and then cut the ribbon. Holding the ends of the ribbon between the thumb and forefinger of your left hand with the loops facing into the palm of your hand, place the end of the covered wire under the ribbon ends at right angles to them. Turn about 6mm (¼in) of the ribbon ends over the wire and pull the wire down in line with the loops before twisting it into the centre of the cut ends of the ribbon loops. Wind it tightly together. Cut the wire about 6mm (¼in) from the end of the ribbon. Make some tails by using only one 5-cm (2-in) loop and leaving 7.5-cm (3-in) tails on either side, wiring in the same way as previously.

To decorate the top of the cake, place a ball of sugarpaste about the size of a small walnut in the centre where the ribbons cross. Flatten it to a dome and use tweezers to push the wired end of the first loop into the centre of the dome. Position four more ribbon loops at right angles to the central loop to form a cross. Fill in the spaces with more loops and tails until none of the sugarpaste dome shows.

BLUE FOR A BOY

Ingredients
fruit cake baked in 17.5-cm (7-in) round cake tin (pan)
boiled, sieved apricot jam or egg white
700g (1½lb) marzipan
sherry or other alcohol
700g (1½lb) sugarpaste
blue dusting colour
brown dusting colour
green dusting colour
red dusting colour
piping gel

Equipment
22.5-cm (9-in) round cake board
rolling pin
sharp knife
2 sheets of rice paper
complete set of food colouring pens
sable paintbrush
sharp pointed scissors
artist's 10-cm (4-in) palette knife
absorbent kitchen paper
1 metre (1 yard) blue double-faced satin ribbon, 6-mm (¼-in) wide
75-cm (24-in) printed christening ribbon

This light-hearted christening cake for a baby boy is inspired by the type of drawings found in children's books and on greeting cards and wrapping paper. Such illustrations have the advantage of simplicity and they are often a suitable size for copying.

Cover the cake with marzipan and sugarpaste and position on the cake board *(see page 12)*.

As this is a quick to decorate cake, the designs *(see page 73)* are traced directly on to rice paper, but they could of course be flooded in royal icing. Make sure that you draw on the shiny smooth side of the rice paper as it is difficult to do so on the other. If the paper has become crinkled through being stored in damp conditions, it is possible to remove the creases with a very cool iron. Be careful not to dry the paper too much or it will become very brittle.

When each outline is completed, fill in the details using an appropriate food colouring pen and, to achieve a soft overall colour, apply a light coating of dusting colour with a dry sable paintbrush. The special dusting colours used by cake decorators have been diluted with cornflour (cornstarch), icing (confectioner's) sugar and other additives to enable them to be easily applied. You can blend the many available colours yourself to create new shades, or add a little cornflour to create tints. Apply the dusting colour with a stippling action. Cut round each outline as

accurately as possible with a pair of sharp pointed scissors. Then coat the back of each design with a thin even layer of piping gel, using an artist's flexible 10-cm (4-in) palette knife. Do not use water to stick the designs in place because rice paper begins to dissolve as soon as it is moistened.

Position the designs directly on to the sugarpaste, pressing them in place with a piece of absorbent kitchen paper to prevent them from smudging.

Tie the narrow blue ribbon round the cake board and then finish the cake by trimming the base with a band of printed christening ribbon, secured with a small dot of royal icing *(see page 21)*.

□ PINK FOR A GIRL □

Ingredients
fruit cake baked in small petal-shaped frame or cake tin (pan)
boiled, sieved apricot jam or egg white
700g (1½lb) marzipan
sherry or other alcohol
900g (2lb) sugarpaste
rose pink food colouring
100g (3½oz) petal paste
royal icing

Equipment
small petal-shaped cake board
rolling pin
sharp knife
cocktail stick (wooden toothpick)
No4 crimper
set of 3 blossom plunger cutters
small and medium heart-shaped plunger cutters
piece of polyurethane foam
sable paintbrush
scriber
vegetable parchment piping bag
No0 nozzle
craft knife with square-ended blade
1.5 metres (1½ yards) pink double-faced satin ribbon, 3-mm (⅛-in) wide

The christening of a baby girl offers the perfect opportunity to decorate a cake daintily. An unusual feature of this cake is the embroidered bib which is laid on the top of the cake.

Cover the cake with marzipan before securing it firmly to the cake board. Colour the sugarpaste with rose pink food colouring and roll out enough to cover both the cake and the board with a single piece of icing. Follow the usual method of covering the cake *(see page 12)* but leave an extra 5cm (2in) all round to enable you to mould the sugarpaste to the bottom edge of the cake and then to flare it out to the edge of the board. Cut round the petal-shaped edge neatly with a sharp knife held vertically. If possible, leave the icing to harden for 48 hours before marking the positions for the embroidery and ribbon insertion. If time is short and you have to start decorating immediately, be very careful since every finger-mark will show while the sugarpaste is soft.

During the drying period, make simple flowers from very thinly rolled petal paste. Hold the blossom plunger cutter between your thumb and second finger and stamp it into the paste. Then hold the cutter just above a piece of polyurethane foam and use your index finger to press the centre of the cutter into it. This releases the paste and at the same time raises the petals. The flowers will retain this shape and quickly dry hard.

Make a template *(see page 74)* of the bib which decorates the top of the cake. The bib is made from two thinly rolled pieces of petal paste, one super-imposed on the other. Both pieces are frilled around their edges. To make the frills, place the point of a cocktail stick (wooden toothpick) about 6mm (¼in) from the edge of the bib. Then rotate the cocktail stick with your index finger, while pressing it into the edge of the petal paste. As you roll the cocktail stick along, the petal paste will pucker, making the edge frilly. Continue all round both pieces of petal paste. Using a No4 crimper, decorate the edge of the frilling and also around the neck of the bib. Using the heart-shaped plunger cutters, stamp out a pattern, following the diagram. Moisten the lower piece with a damp paintbrush and then lay the upper piece on top. Leave for about 8 hours to harden.

When the sugarpaste is hard, mark the positions for the embroidery and ribbon insertion with a scriber, using the template as a guide. With a No0 nozzle, pipe a double row of embroidered scallops and a row of little dots between the marks where the ribbon is to be inserted. Cut some pink satin ribbon into 12-mm (½-in) lengths. Use a craft knife to make incisions in the icing where marked with the scriber, being careful to ensure that they are only just larger than the width of the ribbon. Use the blade of the knife to ease the end of the ribbon into the first of the incisions and then bend it over, using the blade end, and tuck the other end into position. The ribbon will not spring out as there is enough tension across the loop to hold the ends. Repeat this process all round the cake.

Stick the sugar flowers in position below the embroidered band, as illustrated, with small dabs of royal icing. Pipe a dot of pink-coloured royal icing into the centre of each flower. Pipe several dots of icing on the top of the cake and lay the bib in position before writing or piping a message on it. Trim the cake with tiny ribbon bows, secured with beads of icing, at the apex of each of the embroidered scallops.

Baby

ENGAGEMENT CAKE

Ingredients

sponge cake baked in 25-cm (10-in) heart-shaped cake tin (pan)
900g (2lb) sugarpaste
100g (3½oz) petal paste
pink lustre dusting colour
blue lustre dusting colour
royal icing
cornflower blue food colouring
rose pink food colouring

Equipment

35-cm (14-in) heart-shaped cake board
rolling pin
sharp knife
piece of thin card
scissors
spatula or large plastic smoother
vegetable parchment piping bags
No0 nozzle
No6 nozzle
1 metre (1 yard) pink double-faced satin ribbon, 3-mm (⅛-in) wide
1 metre (1 yard) blue double-faced satin ribbon, 3-mm (⅛-in) wide

A traditional Japanese drawing provides the inspiration for the pattern decorating this light sponge cake. It consists of a pair of cranes touching at their wing tips, cut from a very thin layer of white petal paste. The elegance and balance of this design eliminate the need for much additional decoration.

Spread a thin layer of buttercream over the surface of the sponge. Cover the cake with sugarpaste *(see page 12)* and position on the heart-shaped cake board. Alternatively, the cake can be covered with boiled or soft fondant. Whereas sugarpaste is rolled out like pastry, boiled or soft fondant is poured over a cake like syrup.

To make the design for the top of the cake, trace the pattern *(see page 75)* provided on to a template of thin card and cut round the outlines accurately. Roll out the petal paste to about 2mm (1/16in) thick. Lay the card on top and carefully cut round the outlines with a sharp knife, taking care not to split the paste. Using a spatula or large plastic smoother, lift the birds on to the top of the cake. Introduce some subtle shading by carefully dusting the birds with pink and blue lustre dusting colours. Colour a little royal icing with cornflower blue food colouring and using a No0 nozzle, follow the outlines of the stylised wing feathers, the eye and details of the beak of one bird. Colour a little royal icing with rose pink food colouring and repeat the process with the other bird.

Finish the cake by piping a shell border around the base with a No6 nozzle and white royal icing. Attach the pink and blue ribbons around the sides of the cake *(see page 21)*. Trace the letters required for the greeting from the alphabet provided *(see page 15)*. Mark the position on the cake and then pipe the words in either pink- or blue-coloured royal icing with a No0 nozzle.

Congratulations
Sue and Bob
on Your
Engagement

□WEDDING CAKE□

Ingredients

fruit cake baked in small and large scalloped oval tins (pans)
boiled, sieved apricot jam or egg white
1.8kg (4lb) marzipan
sherry or other alcohol
50g (2oz) petal paste
royal icing
cornflour (cornstarch)

Equipment

40-cm (16-in) oval cake board
25-cm (10-in) oval cake board
No2 crimper
slipper mould
cotton wool
sheet of emery paper or an emery board
vegetable parchment piping bags
No0 nozzle
No1 nozzle
36 large ribbon roses
24 small ribbon roses
3 8.75-cm (3½-in) silver-coloured, hollow, octagonal plastic cake pillars
3 wooden dowels or skewers

Every bride wants her cake to be traditional and yet different, which presents quite a challenge to the decorator. The design used for this cake combines these qualities with striking simplicity. The unusual shape of this wedding cake is best described as 'scalloped oval'.

Cover both cakes with marzipan and position on the cake boards. Then cover both cakes with sugarpaste, extending this on to the boards before trimming with a No2 crimper to give a lacy scalloped effect. Leave for about 48 hours for the sugarpaste to harden.

The slipper mould is available from specialist cake decorating shops. Before use, polish it with cotton wool and dust lightly with cornflour (cornstarch). Roll out enough petal paste to fill one part of the two-part mould. Because the heel of the slipper is very slim, completely fill this part of the mould until the petal paste is level with the surface. Line the main part of the mould with a layer of petal paste about 4-mm (3/16-in) thick and press firmly into the mould, trimming the edges neatly. Leave the half slipper to dry for at least 3-4 hours, or preferably overnight. Remove the half slipper from the mould. If the edges are a little rough, rub them gently on a flat sheet of emery paper or file with an emery board. The purpose is to bond both halves of the slipper together eventually without any gaps along the join. Form the second side of the slipper in the same way as the first, then, while the petal paste is still soft, join the hardened side to it with a little royal icing. This will ensure that the slipper comes away from the mould when the second side has dried, as well as making a very good bond between the two parts.

When the slipper is assembled, embellish the entire surface with cornelli work. This is a technique of piping a continuous weaving line of royal icing which creates a filigree effect and also conceals any imperfections in the surface. Using a No0 nozzle, pipe an unbroken line of 'Ms' and 'Ws', making sure that they do not overlap each other. Pipe a 'snail trail' of small teardrops of icing around the top of the slipper with a No1 nozzle and leave to dry for about 1 hour. Fill the cavity with some sugarpaste and arrange small ribbon roses and loops decoratively.

When the sugarpaste on the cakes has hardened, pipe dots with royal icing and a No1 nozzle on the tops and sides of both cakes, following the diagrams *(see page 76)*. Use the template provided as a guide for marking the positions of the ribbon roses on the sides of the cakes. Attach the roses with small dots of royal icing.

Because the icing on the larger cake is too soft to support the weight of the smaller cake, when resting only on pillars, it is important to use the following procedure for arranging the tiers. Accurately measure the distance from the top of the cake board to the top of the larger cake and add 3 mm (1/8 in) to this measurement, plus the length of a plastic pillar. Then cut each wooden dowel or skewer to this length. Mark the position for the base of the pillars within the beading of royal icing already piped on the larger cake, following the diagram. Carefully push the dowels or skewers straight down through the cake until you can feel the resistance of the cake board, then slide the hollow pillars over the dowels — the tip of each should protrude 3mm (1/8in) above the pillar, so that when the upper tier is placed in position, the cake board is resting on the ends of the dowels and is just clear of the plastic pillars. This ensures that no weight is actually pressing on the icing of the lower tier and gives the whole cake stability.

☐CELEBRATION CAKE☐

Ingredients
fruit cake baked in 25-cm (10-in) round cake tin (pan)
boiled, sieved apricot jam or egg white
1.1kg (2½lb) marzipan
sherry or other alcohol
1.8kg (4lb) sugarpaste
Cornish cream food colouring
moss green food colouring
300g (10oz) petal paste
icing (confectioner's) sugar
royal icing

Equipment
40-cm (16-in) round cake board
sheet of gold gift wrap
pastry brush
rolling pin
No1 or No2 crimper
No4 crimper
32.5-cm (13-in) round cake board or plate
piece of board or stiff card
large pins or bent hairpins
scriber or steel knitting needle
vegetable parchment piping bags
No0 nozzle
No1 nozzle
2 metres (2 yards) yellow double-faced satin ribbon, 3-mm (⅛-in) wide
30 large artificial flowers
30 small artificial flowers
5 large artificial leaves
1 metre (1 yard) gold paper banding, 12-mm (½-in) wide

The cake is still a focal point at the reception for a smaller wedding. A single-tier cake can be most impressive and a cake of this type is equally suitable to celebrate other special occasions. This cake takes no longer than 2 hours to decorate, including the upper drape and embroidery.

Cover the cake board with the gold gift wrap. Then cover the cake with marzipan and position on the cake board. Colour the sugarpaste with Cornish cream food colouring, then roll out and cover the cake, extending the sugarpaste on to the board *(see page 12)*. Trim the edge with a No4 crimper. Leave to harden for 48 hours.

To make the drape, mix 300g (10oz) of the sugarpaste with 150g (5oz) of the petal paste and roll out on a flat surface dusted with icing (confectioner's) sugar to 3-mm (⅛-in) thickness. Lay a 32.5-cm (13-in) cake board or plate on the icing and cut round, leaving a border of about 12mm (½in) around it. Using a No1 or No2 crimper, scallop the edge of the circle. Carefully lift the scalloped circle on to a board or piece of stiff card. Brush the top of the cake with some alcohol or water and gently slide the sugarpaste drape from the card over the cake. Try to place it so that it does not require any major repositioning. Don't worry if you don't succeed the first time. Just pick up the icing, form it into a ball, knead it lightly, roll it out and try again! The drape is caught or pleated in six places around its edge. Make a faint mark at each of these points on the cake itself, following the diagram *(see page 77)*. Moisten each point with water, then fold the drape up and secure it with a large pin or bent hairpin until the icing has hardened. While the drape is still soft, use a scriber or steel knitting needle to pierce a series of regularly spaced eyelet holes around the edge. These will form the basis of the embroidery pattern. Leave the cake for 24 hours.

Carefully remove the pins or hairpins from the drape. Then pierce the eyelet holes again with the scriber or knitting needle to define their outlines. Pipe a circle of yellow-coloured royal icing with a No0 nozzle around the circumference of each hole. Repeat twice. A little six-dot flower is piped with the same icing between each set of eyelet holes. Then pipe the stem lines and leaves in green-coloured royal icing with a No0 nozzle. Finish the drape with a scalloped edge of beading, piped with yellow-coloured royal icing and a No1 nozzle. Make six little yellow ribbon bows and fix these to the top of each drape with a dot of royal icing.

To decorate the top of the cake, place a ball of sugarpaste about the size of a small walnut on the centre of the cake and flatten it to a dome. Use tweezers to push the artificial flowers and leaves into position, concealing the sugarpaste dome.

Attach yellow ribbon around the cake *(see page 21)* and place small bouquets of artificial flowers around the base, securing them in the same way as those on the top of the cake. Trim the edge of the cake board with gold paper banding.

□OUR DAY□

Ingredients
fruit cake baked in 15-cm (6-in) square cake tin (pan)
boiled, sieved apricot jam or egg white
700g (1½lb) marzipan
sherry or other alcohol
700g (1½lb) sugarpaste
peach food colouring
violet food colouring
50g (2oz) petal paste
royal icing

Equipment
25-cm (10-in) square cake board
sheet of patterned silver and white gift wrap
rolling pin
sharp knife
4 metres (4 yards) lilac spotted satin ribbon, 3-mm (⅛-in) wide
large-headed pins
No8 crimper
vegetable parchment piping bag
No0 nozzle
No5 nozzle
vase mould
cotton wool
room-scenter candle
3 large peach-coloured artificial roses
4 lilac-coloured artificial lily-of-the-valley
12 dark lilac-coloured small artificial flowers
4 metres (4 yards) peach-coloured double-faced satin ribbon, 6-mm (¼-in) wide

Of all occasions when an anniversary cake may be needed, probably none is more romantic than the first anniversary of a wedding.

Cover the cake board with the patterned gift wrap.

Cover the cake with marzipan. Colour the sugarpaste with peach food colouring, roll it out and cover the cake *(see page 12)*. Place the cake in an offset position on the cake board, so as to leave plenty of space on two sides.

Attach one end of the lilac spotted ribbon 2.5 cm (1in) from the base at the front corner and draw it diagonally across the side of the cake to the back corner, returning diagonally to the front corner, temporarily pinning it before fixing it in position with small dots of royal icing *(see page 21)*. While the sugarpaste is still soft and using the ribbon as a guide, impress a textured effect of embossed hearts over the sides of the cake with a No8 crimper. Take care to arrange the pattern so that its lowest point is at the front of the cake. Then pipe a shell border in peach-coloured royal icing around the base, using a No5 nozzle. Set the cake aside.

A small vase mould, which is available from specialist cake decorating shops, is used to make the candle holder in petal paste *(see page 44)*. If you are unable to obtain such a mould specifically designed for this purpose, use an individual fairy cake baking tin (pan), a fluted brioche tin or even an egg cup. The container needs to be thoroughly clean and to have a larger circumference at the top than at the base, so that it is possible to remove the petal paste after it has hardened. Make two vases, one slightly larger than the other. When they are dry and hard, apply cornelli patterns *(see page 44)* to each with peach-coloured royal icing and a No0 nozzle. Leave to dry before joining them at their bases with a little royal icing to form the candle holder. Place a room-scenter candle in the holder. Fill the space around the candle base with a little sausage of sugarpaste and decorate with artificial flowers. If you like, you can omit the candle and fill the container entirely with flowers.

Roll a crescent-shaped sausage of sugarpaste about 6.25-cm (2½-in) long and 12-mm (½-in) thick and position this just under halfway towards the back corner of the cake. Arrange ribbon loops and tails *(see page 36)* and artificial flowers in the sugarpaste to form a curving spray. Use characters from the alphabet template provided *(see page 15)* for the inscription, piped in violet-coloured royal icing with a No0 nozzle.

Before fixing the decorated candle to the board, attach a small ribbon bow to the front corner of the cake with a dot of royal icing.

To My Wife
on our
First
Anniversary

GRADUATION DAY

Ingredients

sponge cake baked in 30 x 20-cm (12 x 8-in) rectangular cake tin (pan)
1.1kg (2½lb) sugarpaste
Cornish cream food colouring
dark brown food colouring
royal icing

Equipment

35 x 30-cm (14 x 12-in) rectangular cake board
rolling pin
sharp knife
No3 crimper
1.5 metres (1½ yards) dark brown double-faced satin ribbon, 3mm (⅛-in) wide
large-headed pins
vegetable parchment piping bag
No1 nozzle
fine sable paintbrush (optional)
3 sheets of rice paper
2 pieces of wooden dowel, 20-cm (8-in) long
brown food colouring pen

Celebrate graduation day by decorating a cake in academic style with a scroll offering congratulations. Depending on the amount of Cornish cream food colouring that is added to the icing, a variety of shades ranging from a very pale ivory to a deep egg yolk yellow can be obtained.

Place the cake on the board and cover with parchment- or cream-coloured sugarpaste *(see page 12)*, extending it to cover part of the cake board, as illustrated. Trim the edges neatly and within 30 minutes of applying the sugarpaste, use a No3 crimper to form a pattern around the edges of the sugarpaste.

Mark the central point on the length of ribbon by piping a small dot of royal icing. Starting in the centre of the left-hand side of the cake, pin the ribbon in place round the bottom. Proceed round the cake, piping a small dot of icing at 7.5-cm (3-in) intervals and then pinning the ribbon in position. Tie the ends in a bow. When the icing is dry, remove the pins by placing a finger lightly on each side of the pin and twisting it gently before withdrawing it.

Colour a little royal icing with dark brown food colouring and with a No1 nozzle pipe a decoration on the top left and bottom right corners of the cake. A simple design can be piped freehand, or you may prefer to use a template made from the design provided *(see page 80)*. To avoid the necessity of making up any royal icing, the design could be painted on to the freshly covered cake with a fine sable paintbrush and dark brown food colouring. Alternatively, if you allow the surface to harden for at least 24 hours, you could draw the pattern with a brown food colouring pen.

Make the scroll from the rice paper. Using a brown food colouring pen, write the inscription on one sheet. You can use a template made from the alphabet provided *(see page 15)*. With the same food colouring pen, decorate the scroll, using a template made from the design provided, if liked. Attach the remaining sheets of rice paper to the scroll by moistening the top and bottom with a little water. This will give it extra bulk. Then wind each end of the scroll round a piece of dowel. Rice paper can easily be stuck to itself and to the dowels: simply moisten the edge of one sheet and lay it on another. It sticks immediately and permanently. Avoid using too much moisture as there is a danger of the paper dissolving or wrinkling where it has been dampened. Lightly moisten the bottom sheet of rice paper under the dowels before laying the scroll at an angle on top of the cake.

Congratulations
on this
Memorable Day
You are now able to

BE MY VALENTINE

Ingredients
450g (1lb) Madeira cake mixture
1.4kg (3lb) chocolate-flavoured buttercream
buttercream
450g (1lb) sugarpaste
apple green food colouring
Cornish cream food colouring
dark brown food colouring
moss green food colouring
rum or brandy
icing (confectioner's) sugar

Equipment
15-cm (6-in) round cake tin (pan), greased and lined (see method)
15-cm (6-in) wide strip of brown paper
wire cooling rack
sharp serrated knife
5-cm (2-in) round stainless steel biscuit (cookie) cutter
palette knife
cocktail stick (wooden toothpick)
rolling pin
25-cm (10-in) round cake board
No1 crimper
sable paintbrush
piece of muslin
fork
spatula or large plastic smoother
2 sheets of rice paper
black food colouring pen
red food colouring pen
20-cm (8-in) wooden dowel or a wooden skewer

Cupid's arrows tend to land in surprising places and this one has impaled itself in a convenient tree stump!

Line the inside of a 15-cm (6-in) round cake tin (pan) with a brown paper collar, fill with the Madeira cake mixture and bake *(see page 9)*. The purpose of the collar is to allow the cake to rise above the top of the tin without overflowing. Leave in the tin to cool for 5 minutes before turning out on to a wire rack. When the cake is cold, cut a slice across the top at a slight angle with a sharp serrated knife. Use a 5-cm (2-in) round stainless steel biscuit (cookie) cutter to remove a circle of sponge from the slice. Spread a thin even coating of chocolate-flavoured buttercream over the cake, smoothing it with a palette knife. Stick the small circle of sponge against the side of the cake to look like the stump of a branch and coat it with the chocolate-flavoured buttercream. Place the cake in the fridge and leave for 30 minutes for the buttercream to harden.

To make a 'grass' base, marble 175g (6oz) of the sugarpaste with apple and moss green food colourings *(see page 32)* and roll out in a circle. Cover the cake board with the sugarpaste and trim the edge with a No1 crimper.

Colour 125g (4oz) of the sugarpaste with Cornish cream food colouring and roll it out very thinly into a rectangle. Brush the surface with dark brown food colouring, diluted with a little rum or brandy. Cut into strips about 5-cm (2-in) wide. Carefully roll up one strip as if it were a bandage, then add another strip and repeat until all the strips are rolled up together. Trim any rough edges and then cut a 6-mm (¼-in) thick slice across the top. Lay this on a flat surface dusted with icing (confectioner's) sugar, cover with a piece of muslin and roll out very gently until it is the same size as the top of the cake. The muslin prevents the sugarpaste from sticking to the rolling pin and helps to keep the thin circle intact. Make a small disc in the same way for the stump of the branch. Use up any scraps to make 'splinters' for the jagged edge of the tree stump.

Stick the two discs of sugarpaste in position on the cake with a little uncoloured buttercream, then stick the splinters in position. Spread a thick layer of chocolate-flavoured buttercream over the sides of the cake, taking care not to get any on to the top. Roughen the surface with the back of a fork to suggest a pattern of uneven bark. Place a dab of uncoloured buttercream in the centre of the grass, then carefully lift the cake on a spatula or large plastic smoother into position on the cake board.

Cut the flight for Cupid's arrow from rice paper, marking the quills with a black food colouring pen, and attach to a 20-cm (8-in) wooden dowel or a wooden skewer *(see page 50)*. Write the message boldly with a red food colouring pen on a piece of rice paper and secure it to the cake with the arrow.

If you like, you can pipe green-coloured buttercream around the base of the tree trunk, using a No1 nozzle, to represent grass. You could also add a few flowers, a toadstool or even a marzipan frog hoping to be turned into Prince Charming if kissed by a passing princess!

FIONA...
BE MY
VALENTINE!

FATHER'S DAY

Ingredients
sponge or light fruit cake baked in 20 x 15-cm (8 x 6-in) rectangular cake tin (pan)
buttercream
1.6kg (3½lb) sugarpaste
black food colouring
dark brown food colouring
red food colouring
skintone food colouring
piping gel
300g (10oz) petal paste

Equipment
45 x 30-cm (18 x 12-in) cake board
sheet of brown gift wrap
sharp serrated knife
palette knife
rolling pin
thin spatula
flexible plastic smoother
ruler or straight edge
sable paintbrush
sheet of rice paper
complete set of food colouring pens
No6 crimper
sharp knife
cotton wool
wadding

This unusual design for a father's day cake gives plenty of scope for making amusing drawings on the cards, which are displayed on the mantelpiece.

Cover the cake board with the brown gift wrap. Cut the top of the cake level with a sharp serrated knife before coating the entire surface with a thin layer of buttercream. Place in the fridge and leave for 30 minutes for the buttercream to harden.

Colour some sugarpaste brick brown with red and dark brown food colouring, roll it out and cover the top and three sides of the cake, leaving one long side uncovered *(see page 12)*. Turn the cake over on to a clean and crumb-free flat surface, spread a layer of buttercream over the original base and then cover this with sugarpaste. Carefully seal the joins between the sides and the original base. Lift the cake on a thin spatula and carefully stand the cake on its uncoated edge at the back of the covered cake board. Use a flexible plastic smoother to retouch any marks in the sugarpaste and to ensure that the corners and edges are as sharply defined as possible.

Use the side of a ruler or straight edge to mark the lines of mortar between the simulated bricks of the sides of the fireplace *(see page 77)*. Paint a semicircular fireback with black food colouring to simulate soot. While this is drying, colour a small quantity of sugarpaste brick red with skintone and red food colourings and roll it into a thin strip, 18-mm (¾-in) wide and 4-cm (10-in) long. Moisten one side and mould it into an arch against the fireplace. Use the back of a knife to indent the sugarpaste to represent tiles and do not forget to add an extra piece of sugarpaste at the centre of the arch for the keystone. If the edges of the tiles have become a little torn as a result of stretching the sugarpaste into a semicircle, roll a very thin strip of sugarpaste like a shoelace and stick it against the tiles with a little water.

Draw glowing coals and flames on rice paper with food colouring pens, then cut out the shapes and stick them against the black fireback with piping gel. Roll out some more of the brick red-coloured sugarpaste to form a hearth with tiles and a hearth rail. Trim the edge with a No6 crimper and place in position.

To make the greeting cards, roll out the petal paste very thinly and cut into rectangles. These are then folded and supported until they are dry to prevent them closing. Use petal paste also for making the mantelpiece, which could be marbled *(see page 32)*. Carefully cut out a rectangle slightly larger than the top of the cake, leave to dry and then stick in position with royal icing or buttercream.

When the greeting cards are quite dry, sketch your designs using a set of food colouring pens. To prevent the cards from being damaged as you work, lay them on a thick pad of cotton wool and put some extra wadding between the front and back, so that they are less liable to snap along the fold.

Because this cake is standing on its side and not on its original base, it is essential that the cake board is always kept level.

You win! Happy Day
HAPPY BIRTHDAY DAD
A Gift For You

EASTER BONNET

Ingredients
sponge cakes baked in 30-cm (12-in) round flan tin (pan) and half of a small spherical tin
buttercream
1.1kg (2½lb) marzipan
dark brown food colouring
rose pink food colouring

Equipment
30-cm (12-in) round cake board
palette knife
sharp serrated knife
rolling pin
plastic wrap
No1 crimper
6 large artificial flowers
5 small artificial leaves
45-cm (18-in) pink lacelon ribbon

This cake revives the pleasant old custom of ladies having a new bonnet for Easter, to mark the beginning of spring weather.

Spread a layer of buttercream evenly over the top and sides of the round sponge. Use a sharp serrated knife to level the top of the sponge baked in half of the spherical tin (pan), then position it with the domed side uppermost at the back of the round sponge. Spread buttercream over the domed sponge and seal the join where it rests on the round one. Place the cake in the fridge and leave for at least 30 minutes for the buttercream to harden.

Reserve 75g (3oz) of the marzipan and divide the remainder into one-third and two-thirds portions. Roll out the larger portion in a circle measuring about 30cm (12in) in diameter, then cover with plastic wrap to prevent the surface drying out. Colour the smaller portion with dark brown food colouring and roll into a long sausage. Then flatten it and roll it out very thinly into a rectangle. Bend open a No1 crimper and use it to cut a scalloped band from the marzipan, tapering it from just over 2.5-cm (1-in) wide at one end to 12-mm (½-in) at the other. Repeat this process until you have cut eight bands. Moisten the back of each band with water and starting from the centre, position them like the folds of a fan across the circle of white marzipan, tapering them until the brown scalloped bands almost meet at one edge. When all the bands are in positon, lay a muslin cloth over the surface and use a rolling pin to press the two colours together and inlay the brown into the white. When the surface is smooth and the inlaid marzipan is large enough to cover the cake, pick it up and lay it in place. Make sure that as the marzipan is moulded to the contours of the crown of the hat, any distortions follow the direction of the scalloped bands. Finish the brim by making a scalloped edge with a No1 crimper.

Cut the reserved white marzipan in half and colour one half with rose pink food colouring. Roll each portion into a long sausage about the thickness of a pencil. Loosely twist them together to form a cord to tie around the crown of the hat. A frivolous spray of lacelon ribbon, artificial leaves and artificial flowers is used to decorate the top of the hat. Push the stems into a piece of leftover marzipan and stick on to the side of the cake.

UNCOOKED MARZIPAN

This traditional marzipan tends to be a little like short pastry when it is rolled out – slightly oily and crumbly. As it is uncooked, it is not advisable to store it, even in a refrigerator, for more than two or three days, well covered in plastic wrap. It can, however, be frozen for up to six months.

450g (1lb) caster (superfine) sugar, sifted
450g (1lb) icing (confectioner's) sugar, sifted
450g (1lb) ground almonds
1 teaspoon rum, brandy or whisky
2 large or 3 small eggs (or 4 egg yolks), lightly beaten

Combine the two sugars, add the ground almonds and mix thoroughly. Make a well in the centre and add the alcohol, which acts as a preservative. Gradually add sufficient lightly beaten egg until the mixture forms a stiff paste. You may not need all the egg. Turn the mixture out on to a flat surface that has been dusted with icing (confectioner's) sugar and knead lightly until the marzipan becomes smooth. Do not overwork the mixture, or it will become very greasy as the almond oil is released.

EASTER RABBIT

Ingredients
fruit cake baked in 15-cm (6-in) round cake tin (pan)
boiled, sieved apricot jam or egg white
700g (1½lb) marzipan
sherry or other alcohol
450g (1lb) sugarpaste
black food colouring
brown food colouring
pink food colouring
pink dusting colour
150g (5 oz) petal paste
royal icing

Equipment
17.5-cm (7-in) round cake board
rolling pin
pastry brush
sharp knife
10-cm (4-in) round pastry cutter
scissors
sable paintbrush
vegetable parchment piping bags
No1 nozzle
No5 nozzle
small chocolate Easter eggs
cocktail sticks (wooden toothpicks)
selection of party tapers or birthday candles
50cm (20in) navy satin ribbon, 2.5-cm (1-in) wide
1.5 metres (1½ yards) pink double-faced satin ribbon, 3-mm (⅛-in) wide

Inspired perhaps by the famous conjuring trick, the Easter rabbit is emerging from the crown of a top hat, its brim decorated with traditional small eggs and burning candles.

Cover the cake with marzipan and build up the perimeter of the top of the cake by adding a rim of marzipan. Make a ring of marzipan, 15-cm (6-in) in diameter and 2.5-cm (1-in) thick, and stick around the top of the cake with a little sherry or other alcohol. Smooth the join at the side and flatten the top. Leave the cake for 24 hours for the marzipan to harden.

Colour the sugarpaste grey with black food colouring *(see page 12)*. To achieve a very smooth finish, roll out the sugarpaste to form a strip measuring 17.5-cm (7-in) wide, 52.5-cm (21-in) long and about 6-mm (¼-in) thick. Turn the strip over, moisten it with alcohol and then roll the marzipan-covered cake along it, picking up the sugarpaste as the cake turns. The point where the ends meet becomes the back of the cake. Trim this join and the top and bottom edges with a sharp knife. Then turn the cake on to its base again and position on the board.

Colour the petal paste grey with black food colouring, then roll it out to about 3mm (⅛in) thick. Use the template provided to cut out a 20-cm (8-in) oval, then remove the centre with a 10-cm (4-in) round pastry cutter. Leave the petal paste to harden for 24 hours and then fix it in position on the top of the cake.

To make the rabbit, start by forming a piece of marzipan into the size and shape of a pear. Stand it on its thick end and, starting at the thin end, make a vertical cut down the centre to about halfway. Bend the two sections outwards to form the ears. Hollow them slightly at the front, then give them pointed tips. Mould the area below the ears to suggest the eye sockets and cheeks. Pinch the cheeks to simulate spiky whiskers and snip the ends with scissors.

Use up the remaining marzipan to make the forepaws by rolling two balls about the size of large hazelnuts into cone shapes. Partially flatten one end of each between the finger and thumb, and make three indentations in the ends to indicate the position of the claws. Bend the paws at an angle so that they will fit over the brim of the upturned top hat. Leave the head to dry before painting the inside of the ears with pink food colouring and dusting with pink dusting colour. Then pipe small stars of royal icing with a No5 nozzle over the head, excluding the nose and the insides of the ears. Fill the eye sockets with white royal icing and when dry, pipe the eyeballs with brown-coloured royal icing. Dust the nose with pink dusting colour.

Position the rabbit inside the hat and arrange a forepaw on its brim on each side of the head. Fill the remaining space inside the hat with chocolate Easter eggs, skewering some on cocktail sticks to suggest balloons.

Place a few more chocolate Easter eggs around the brim. Stick some party tapers or birthday candles at angles directly into the marzipan at the base of the rabbit. Trim the hat with 2.5-cm (1-in) wide navy ribbon just below the brim *(see page 21)*, and lay some 3-mm (⅛-in) wide pink satin ribbon over the navy band and around the base of the cake to add extra highlights.

Lindt

SNOWY MOUNTAINS

Ingredients
3.5kg (7lb) fruit cake mixture
boiled, sieved apricot jam or egg white
1.6kg (3½lb) marzipan
sherry or other alcohol
3kg (6lb) sugarpaste
royal icing

Equipment
large and small tiffin or bell-shaped cake tins (pans)
30 x 45-cm (12 x 18-in) rectangular cake board
pastry brush
rolling pin
No2 crimper
palette knife
assorted plastic Christmas ornaments

You don't have to ice a landscaped masterpiece to have fun making this unusual cake. Just watch the children's faces when they see it on the Christmas tea table. You can use figures and trees similar to those illustrated, or perhaps include a model of a vintage car overturned in a snowdrift, or igloos and polar bears for an Arctic effect – indeed anything that adds to the wintry landscape.

Brush the tins (pans) with melted fat and sprinkle them with flour, or spray with a special non-stick aerosol. Bake 2.6kg (5lb) of the fruit cake mixture in the large bell-shaped tin and 900g (2lb) in the small one. Turn the cakes out while still warm and leave overnight to cool. Brush the cakes with apricot jam or egg white, then cover with marzipan. Position

the larger cake in one corner of the cake board with the smaller one closer to the centre. Brush the marzipan with sherry or other alcohol. If you have any spare pieces of marzipan or sugarpaste, attach them to the cake board to form irregularly shaped hummocks or mounds to add interest to the terrain. Add a 'sausage' of marzipan to the side of the dish for the ski-run.

Roll out a very large piece of sugarpaste in a rectangle measuring about 50 x 62.5cm (20 x 25 in) and 6-mm (¼-in) thick. Drape it over the cakes and board, and start moulding, first pressing the paste into the area between the two cakes. Make sure that this is completed before adjusting the paste on either side and moulding it around the domed top of each cake. Because some of the sugarpaste will subsequently be covered with royal icing, it is not necessary to achieve a smooth covering, but it is important to try to make a good join between the sugarpaste and the cakes, the board and the little hummocks. Trim the edges with a No2 crimper.

Spread royal icing generously over the top of each mountain. Working with the flat side of a palette knife, dab the icing and pull it up and out into rough peaks or icicles. Spread some royal icing over the hummocks and around the sides of the mountains, at the same time roughing it up into small peaks. Complete the ski-run by coating it with icing and then making parallel tracks in it. Coat the entire cake in this way, using your imagination to add interesting features. Arrange a selection of appropriate Christmas and wintry ornaments to help create a colourful scene.

JINGLE BELLS

Ingredients
fruit cake baked in 20-cm (8-in) round cake tin (pan)
boiled, sieved apricot jam or egg white
900g (2lb) marzipan
sherry or other alcohol
900g (2lb) sugarpaste
about 5ml (1 tsp) egg white, lightly beaten
225g (8oz) caster (superfine) sugar
green sparkle colour
red dusting colour
silver lustre dusting colour
royal icing
Christmas red food colouring

Equipment
30-cm (12-in) round cake board
rolling pin
pastry brush
scriber or sharp-pointed needle
No9 crimper or holly-shaped cutter
mixing bowl
bell mould
cotton wool
knife
sable paintbrushes
black food colouring pen
green food colouring pen
red food colouring pen
bell-shaped metal stencil
vegetable parchment piping bags
No0 nozzle
No42 nozzle
3 metres (3 yards) red double-faced satin ribbon, 6-mm (1/4-in) wide
3 metres (3 yards) green double-faced satin ribbon, 6-mm (1/4-in) wide
florist's wire

There is so much to prepare during the festive season that sugarpaste, being so quick to apply, is the obvious choice for covering the cake. Plain white sugar bells bound with red and green ribbons and a colourful stencilled bell linked with a chain of holly make a sophisticated decoration for a Christmas cake.

Cover the cake with marzipan, then sugarpaste *(see page 12)*. Before the surface of the icing has begun to harden, use a scriber to mark the positions where the bells will be stencilled on the sides of the cake. Then, with a No9 crimper or holly-shaped cutter, lightly impress the outline of the holly chain into the sugarpaste, but do not press through the coating to the marzipan beneath. Impress the positions for the holly berries with a scriber. Leave the cake for 24 hours for the sugarpaste to harden.

The sugar bells are made from a mixture of egg white and caster (superfine) sugar. Put the lightly beaten egg white in a bowl and add the caster sugar, mixing very thoroughly until the sugar has the consistency of wet sand. If it feels too dry, add a little more egg white and if it is too wet, a little more sugar. To make coloured bells, simply add a little food colouring, mixing it in evenly. The bell mould is available from specialist cake decorating shops. Dry and polish the inside of the mould with cotton wool, then pack it firmly with the caster sugar until it is completely full. Level off any unevenness with the back of a knife, then tap the edge of the mould sharply against a flat surface and the solid mass of sugar will drop out. Wash and thoroughly dry the inside of the mould and repeat the process for the second sugar bell. Leave the solid sugar shapes to dry for about 1 hour or until the bells are firm enough to be picked up. Then very carefully scrape the sugar from the centres while it is still moist. It may be necessary to check the drying rate of the bells at regular intervals before beginning to hollow them, as the speed at which they harden depends on the humidity and temperature of your kitchen. If they are allowed to become too hard, it is difficult to remove the insides. If this happens, heat a metal skewer and burn a hole right down through the centre, then thread them on a ribbon and hang them on the Christmas tree. Make the bells as thin as possible without breaking them. You can re-use the moist sugar removed from the centres to make more bells. Leave them to dry out completely before assembling them on the cake.

Complete the holly leaves on the side of the cake by carefully dusting the shapes with a little green sparkle colour applied with a soft dry paintbrush. Highlight the holly berries by making dots with a red food colouring pen, or with red-coloured royal icing at the time when you pipe your Christmas greeting on the top of the cake.

The principal decoration on the side of the cake is the green- and red-coloured stencilled bell. A stencil cut from card or stiff paper is quite adequate, but here a fine white enamelled metal stencil, sold as a Christmas tree hanging ornament, has been used. Trace its outline with a black food colouring pen. Continue to hold it in place against the icing and use a fairly stiff paintbrush to stipple through the pattern with red dusting colour. If you use a solid stencil, you will of course need to move it and add the details by drawing, painting or flooding with icing.

To complete the cake, pipe a shell border with a No42 nozzle and royal icing around the base of the cake. Secure the sugar bells in position on the top of the cake with a little royal icing. Place a small dome of sugarpaste between the sugar bells at the back of the cake and finish with a flourish of red and green ribbon loops *(see page 36)*. Make a clapper for each sugar bell from a piece of sugarpaste the size of a hazelnut and fix this on to a piece of florist's wire. Dust the clappers with silver lustre powder. Pipe a Christmas greeting with a No0 nozzle and red-coloured royal icing, using letters from the alphabet template provided *(see page 15)*.

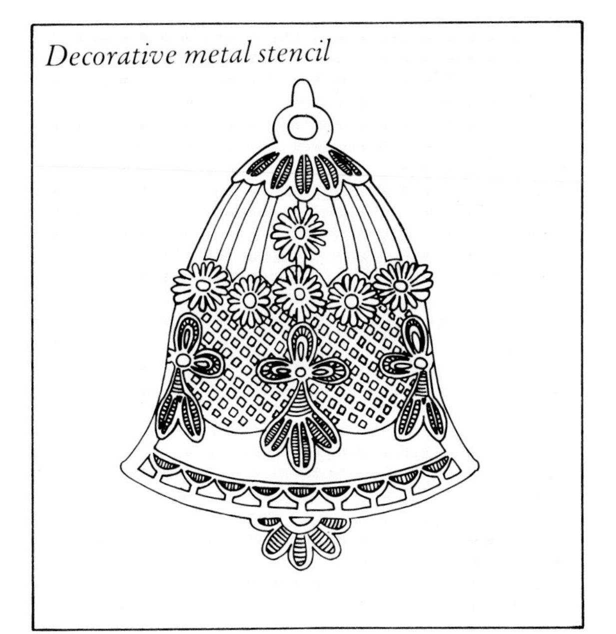
Decorative metal stencil

□CHRISTMAS STORY□

Ingredients

fruit cake baked in multi-size cake tin (pan) set at 30 x 20-cm (12 x 8-in) with book insert
boiled, sieved apricot jam or egg white
1.1kg (2½lb) marzipan
sherry or other alcohol
1.4kg (3lb) sugarpaste
piping gel
Christmas red food colouring
royal icing
dusting colours

Equipment

45 x 30-cm (18 x 12-in) cake board
sharp knife
pastry brush
rolling pin
plastic scraper, smoother or straight edge
2 sheets of rice paper
complete set of food colouring pens
soft sable paintbrush
No2 crimper
scissors
absorbent kitchen paper
3 red sugar poinsettias
3 large sugar Christmas roses
4 small sugar Christmas roses
50cm (20in) red satin ribbon, 2.5-cm (1-in) wide

Although this cake was originally created for Christmas, the design is equally suitable for other occasions such as a confirmation or ordination.

Cover the cake with marzipan, moulding the top to resemble an open book, then cover with sugarpaste *(see page 12)*. Position on the cake board, as shown in the illustration. Before the sugarpaste becomes hard, make a series of parallel indentations along the sides of the cake to represent the edges of the pages, pressing into the icing with the edge of a plastic scraper, a smoother or a straight edge. Repeat this process on the top and bottom edges of the cake, or, as in the cake illustrated here, draw a series of lines on to rice paper and stick this to the sugarpaste with piping gel. As rice paper is edible, use food colouring pens rather than ordinary felt-tip pens.

Colour 225 (8oz) of the sugarpaste with Christmas red food colouring and leave for 30 minutes. Strong colours take a little time to develop their full brightness after they have been mixed into icing. Then roll out the red-coloured sugarpaste and cut it into narrow strips. Stick these around the base of the cake with a little water or alcohol. Mitre the corners to make neat joins and trim the edges with a sharp knife. Crimp round the edges with a No2 crimper to give the impression of an expensive binding of tooled leather.

The design used on the left-hand page of the book was taken from a section of a Victorian stained glass window. Use the template *(see page 79)* provided to trace this on to

rice paper and colour with the appropriate food colouring pens. The pale tints between the dark lines are produced by applying dry dusting colours with a soft sable paintbrush *(see page 38).* Cut out the completed design, spread an even coating of piping gel very thinly over the back of the rice paper and smooth it into place on the sugarpaste, using a sheet of absorbent kitchen paper so that you don't smudge the colours.

The floral arrangement on the right-hand page consists of sugar flowers, which are available from specialist cake decorating shops, and delicate fronds of pine needles. The fronds are drawn directly on to the icing with green, yellow and brown food colouring pens, following the diagram. For other occasions these could be replaced by any appropriate design. Stick the flowers in place with little dabs of royal icing. No piping is necessary for this cake.

Finish the cake by laying two strips of 2.5-cm (1-in) wide red satin ribbon down the centre fold of the book and cutting the ends to form fishtails.

☐HAPPY NEW YEAR☐

Ingredients

sponge cake baked in 30 x 10-cm (12 x 4-in) rectangular cake tin (pan) or multi-size tin set at 10-cm (4-in)
1.4kg (3lb) praline-flavoured buttercream
liqueur
black food colouring
Christmas red food colouring
pink food colouring
royal icing

Equipment

30-cm (12-in) universal cake board
sharp serrated knife
pastry brush
palette knife
serrated scraper
30-cm (12-in) disposable plastic piping bags
No0 nozzle
No2 nozzle
No4 nozzle
No12 nozzle
No58 nozzle

People have consumed so much Christmas fare that by the time New Year's Eve arrives, they are ready for something different. This cake could be decorated in royal icing but for speed and convenience buttercream is strongly recommended.

Cut through the centre of the sponge with a sharp serrated knife. Brush both cut surfaces with liqueur, spread with some praline-flavoured buttercream and sandwich the two pieces together again. Position the cake on the board and cover with a very thin layer of the buttercream. Put it in the fridge and leave for 30 minutes for the buttercream to harden. Then apply another thicker layer of buttercream. Draw a serrated scraper over the top of the cake, moving the scraper from left to right so that undulating lines appear. Hold the scraper vertically as you comb the sides, starting and stopping at each corner. Using a No12 nozzle, pipe a heavy scroll of buttercream around both the top and bottom edges of the cake.

When making any pressure-piped figures, it is important to maintain an even pressure on the piping bag, and to draw the nozzle away from the starting point so slowly that its tip remains in the expelled icing until the pressure on the piping bag is eased. Unless you wish to make thin lines, do not attempt to pull the icing as you ease the pressure on the bag at the end of any movement. The most important principle in pressure-piped figures is to pay attention to the anatomy of the creatures involved. It may appear obvious but the basic rules about the angles in which the different joints actually bend must be followed.

Colour some of the buttercream with pink food colouring and fill a 30-cm (12-in) plastic piping bag fitted with a No4 nozzle to make the elephants *(see page 80)*. Hold the bag vertically and, with heavy pressure, form a large ball, then reduce the pressure slightly and while bringing the nozzle closer to the surface of the cake, move it forward to form the front end of the large, pear-shaped body. Remember that the tip of the nozzle must

remain in the icing. At this stage the 'elephant-to-be' could be made to lie in any position – on its side, its back or its stomach with its legs splayed out – as the same pear-shaped body is the basis for many variations.

Make the elephant's legs with the same basic movement, by placing the tip of the nozzle against the body, putting pressure on the piping bag and drawing the nozzle away steadily. Slacken the pressure, pull the nozzle to one side of the leg and move it in a small circle to form a blunt end which becomes the foot. Release the pressure completely – the buttercream will instantly stop coming out of the nozzle – and draw the bag away gently without disturbing the icing.

Make the elephant's head by piping a large ball of buttercream at the tapered end of the body. When the ball is large enough, release some of the pressure and then draw the nozzle away, moving it from left to right to form the trunk.

With very light pressure, pipe the tail in the shape of a teardrop, the widest part being that attached to the body.

Pipe the ears with a No58 nozzle which must be inclined at an angle and pivoted through a half-turn to make the curved shape of the elephant's ears. Pipe the elephant's toes and tusks with a No2 nozzle and white royal icing. Use black-coloured royal icing and a No0 nozzle for adding the details of the elephant's eyes. Make two more elephants in the same way, adding interest by varying their positions.

Complete the decoration of this cake by piping a New Year greeting with red-coloured buttercream and a No2 nozzle.

Templates for Chico the Clown (see pages 22-23)

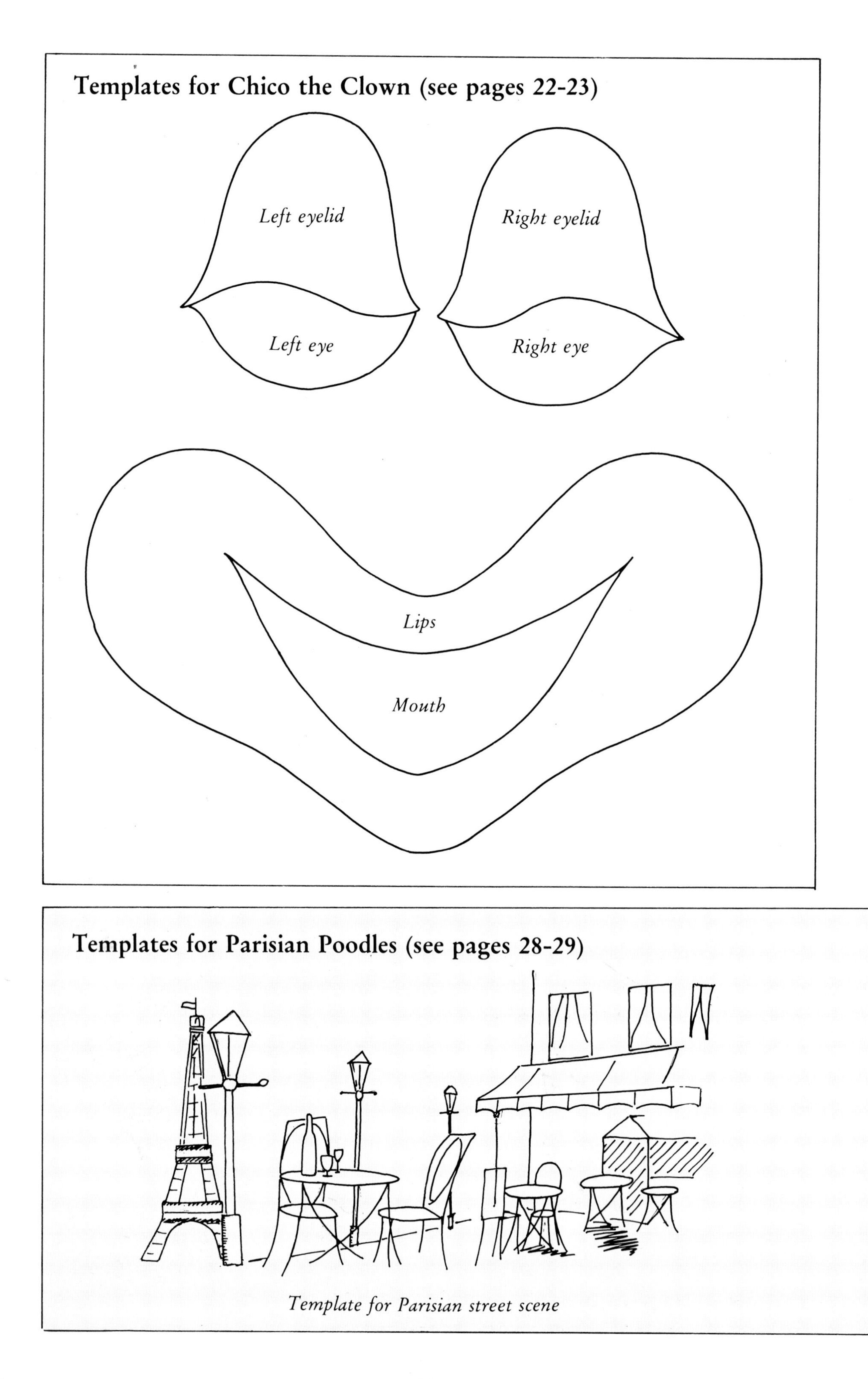

Templates for Parisian Poodles (see pages 28-29)

Template for Parisian street scene

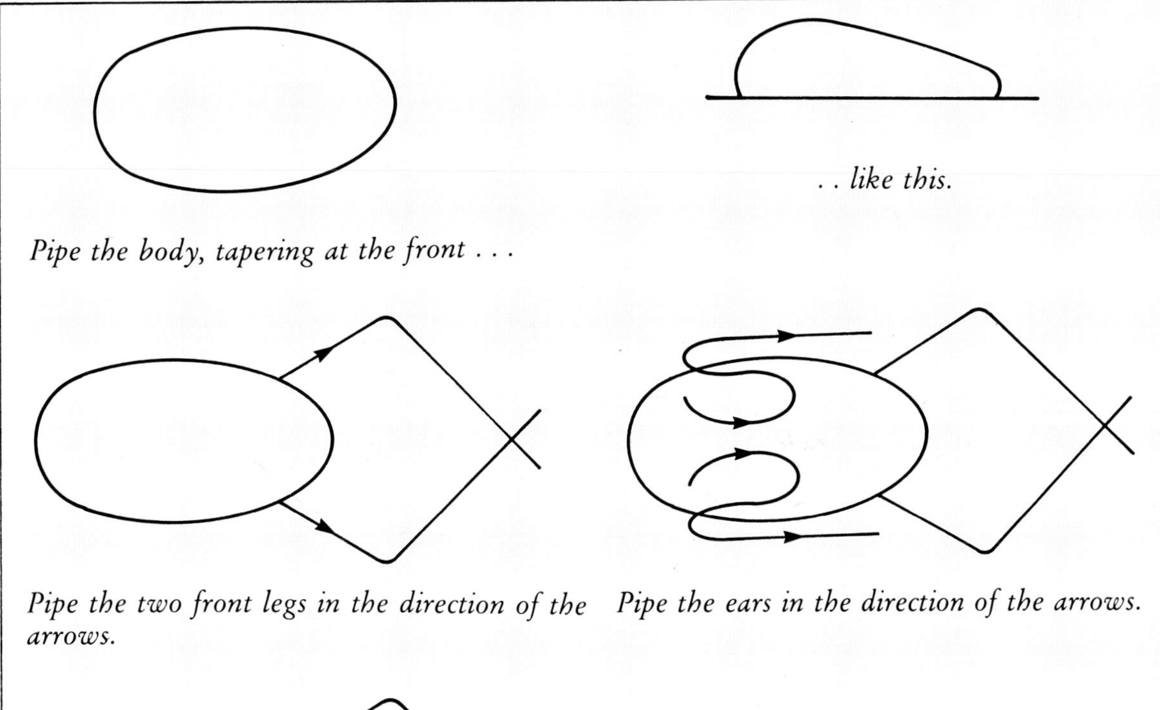

Pipe the body, tapering at the front . . .

. . like this.

Pipe the two front legs in the direction of the arrows.

Pipe the ears in the direction of the arrows.

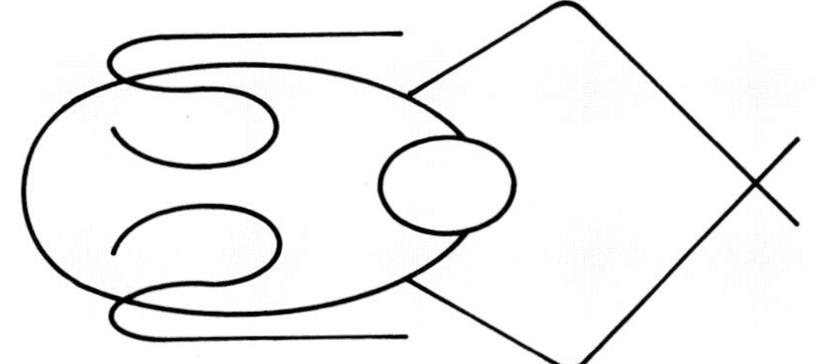

Finally pipe the neck and muzzle and a little more on top for the topknot.

Pipe the body tapering off at the head.

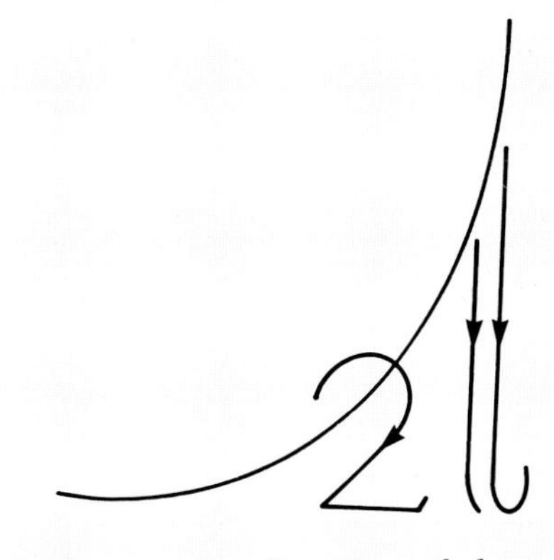

Pipe the legs in the direction of the arrows.

Pipe the ears and muzzle.

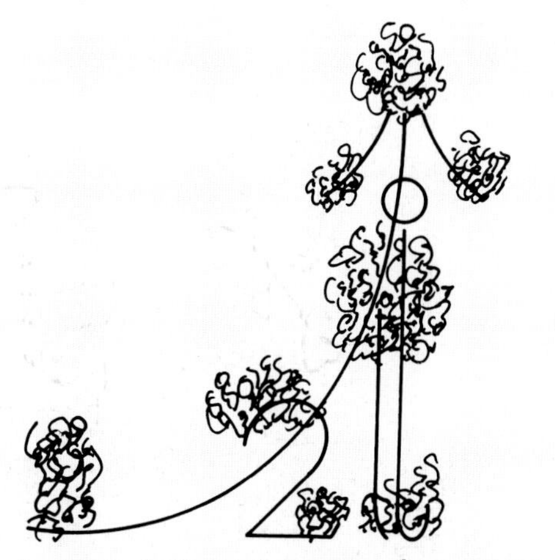

Pipe the curly hair and details of eyes, muzzle and topknot.

Templates for Orchid Cake (see pages 30-31)

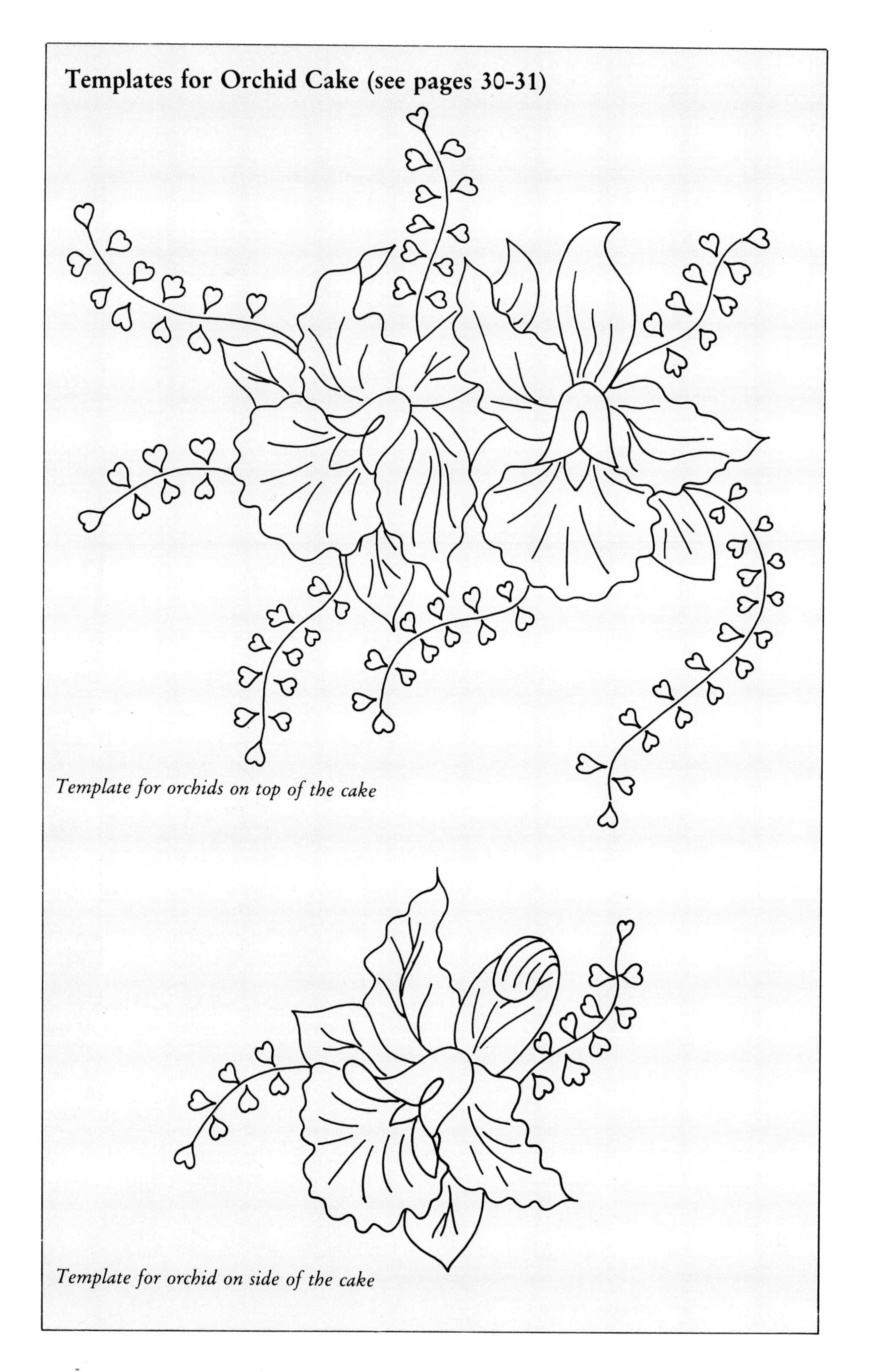

Template for orchids on top of the cake

Template for orchid on side of the cake

Templates for Carpenter's Cake (see pages 32-33)

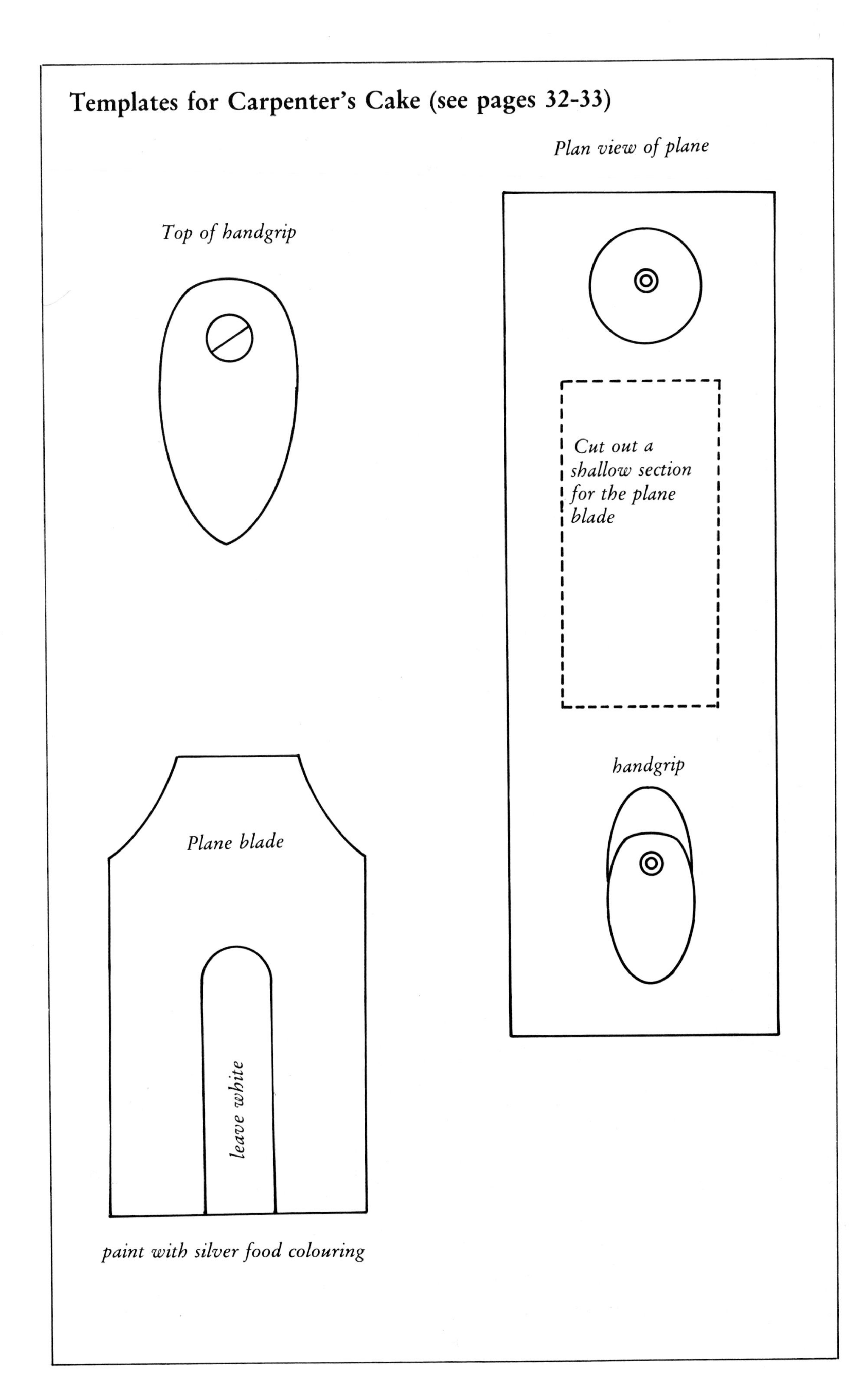

Templates for Smile Please (see pages 34-35)

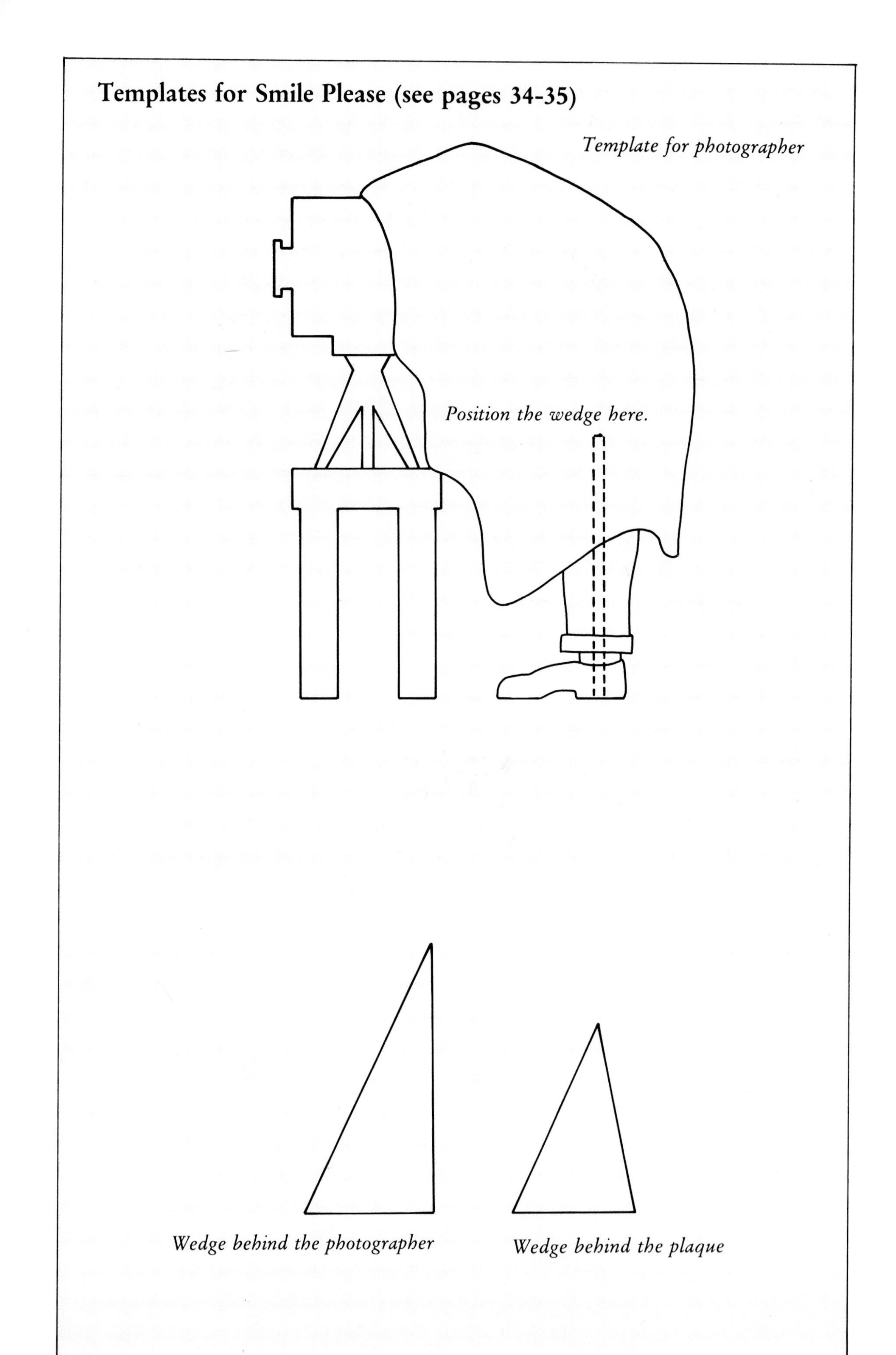

Templates for Blue for a Boy (see pages 38-39)

Selection of designs

Templates for Pink for a Girl (see pages 40-41)

Template for baby's bib, with dotted line indicating position for crimper work.

Template for curve of piping and ribbon insertion positions on side of cake.

Template for Engagement Cake (see pages 42-43)

Template for birds

Templates for Wedding Cake (see pages 44–45)

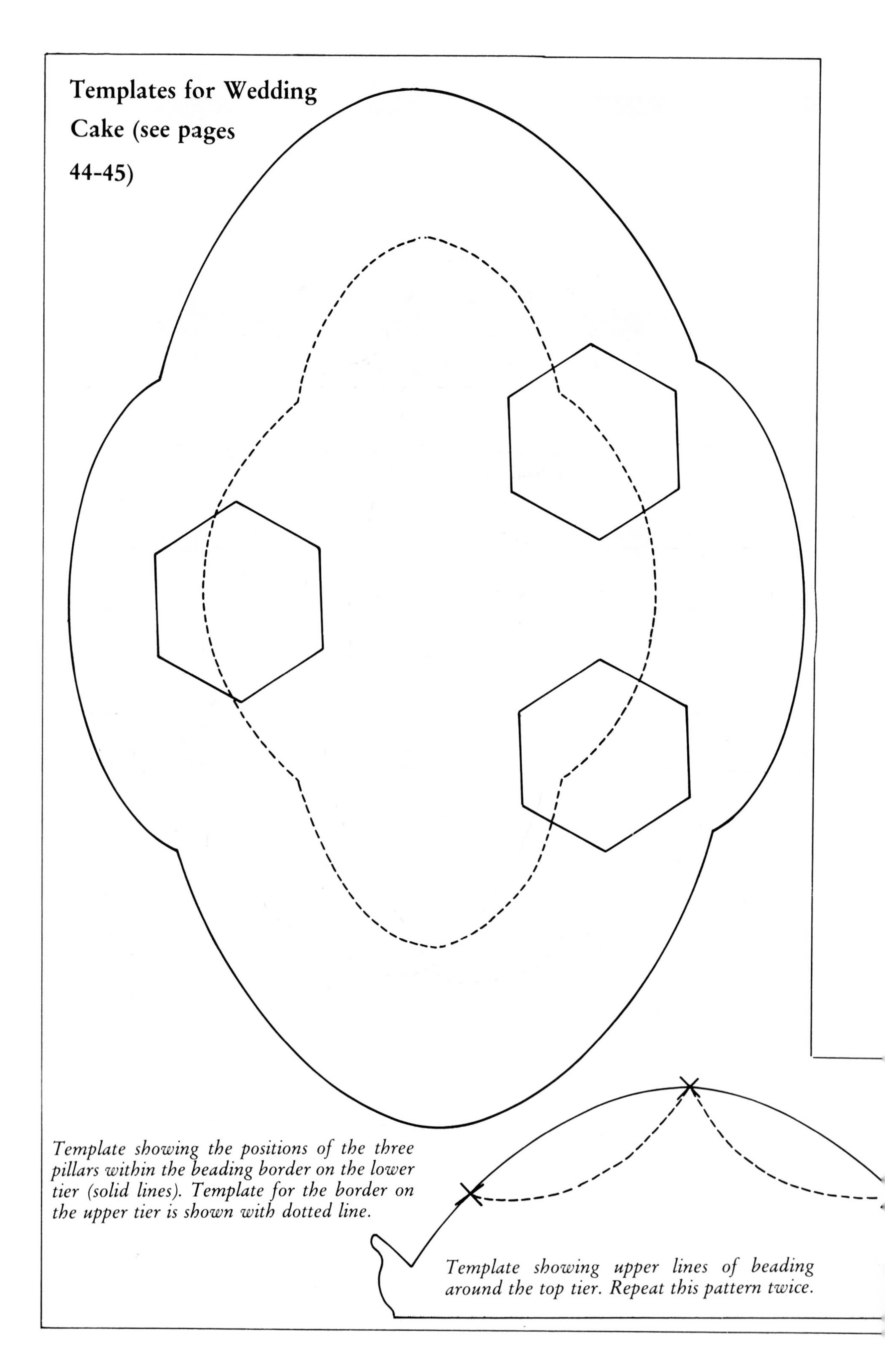

Template showing the positions of the three pillars within the beading border on the lower tier (solid lines). Template for the border on the upper tier is shown with dotted line.

Template showing upper lines of beading around the top tier. Repeat this pattern twice.

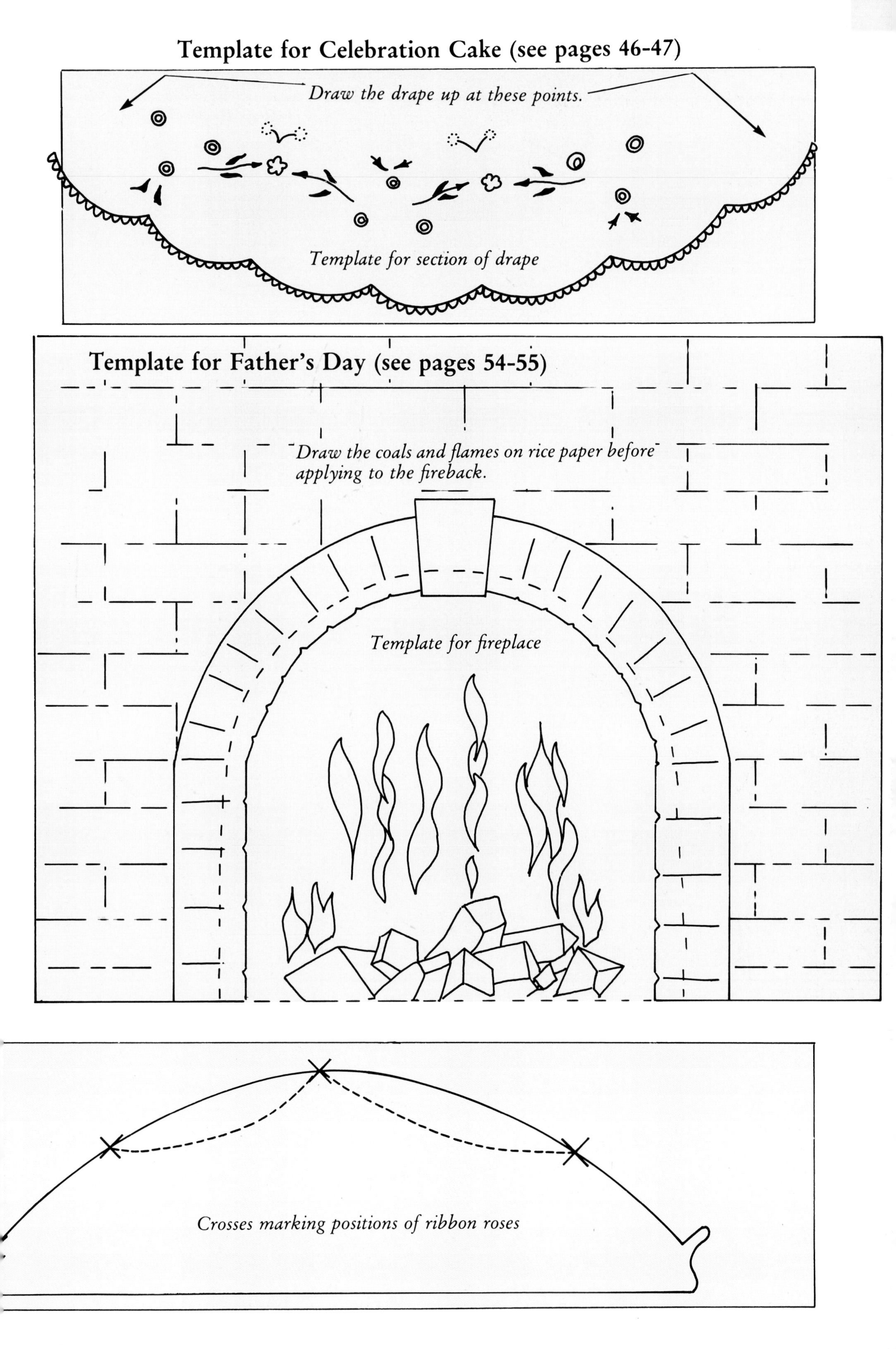

Template for Celebration Cake (see pages 46-47)
Draw the drape up at these points.
Template for section of drape
Template for Father's Day (see pages 54-55)
Draw the coals and flames on rice paper before applying to the fireback.
Template for fireplace
Crosses marking positions of ribbon roses

Template for Easter Rabbit (see pages 58-59)

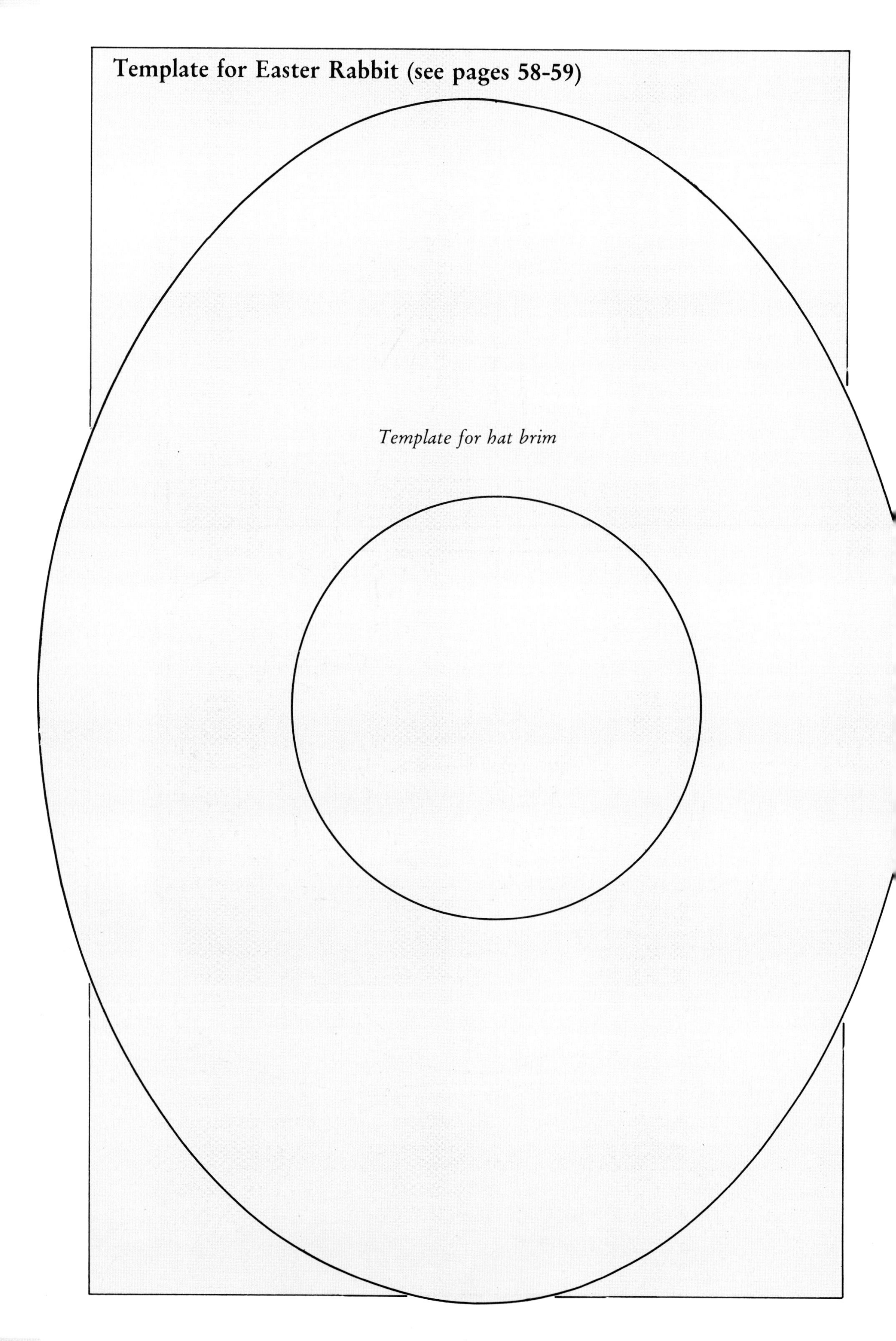

Templates for Christmas Story
(see pages 64-65)

Template for stained glass window

Pine fronds

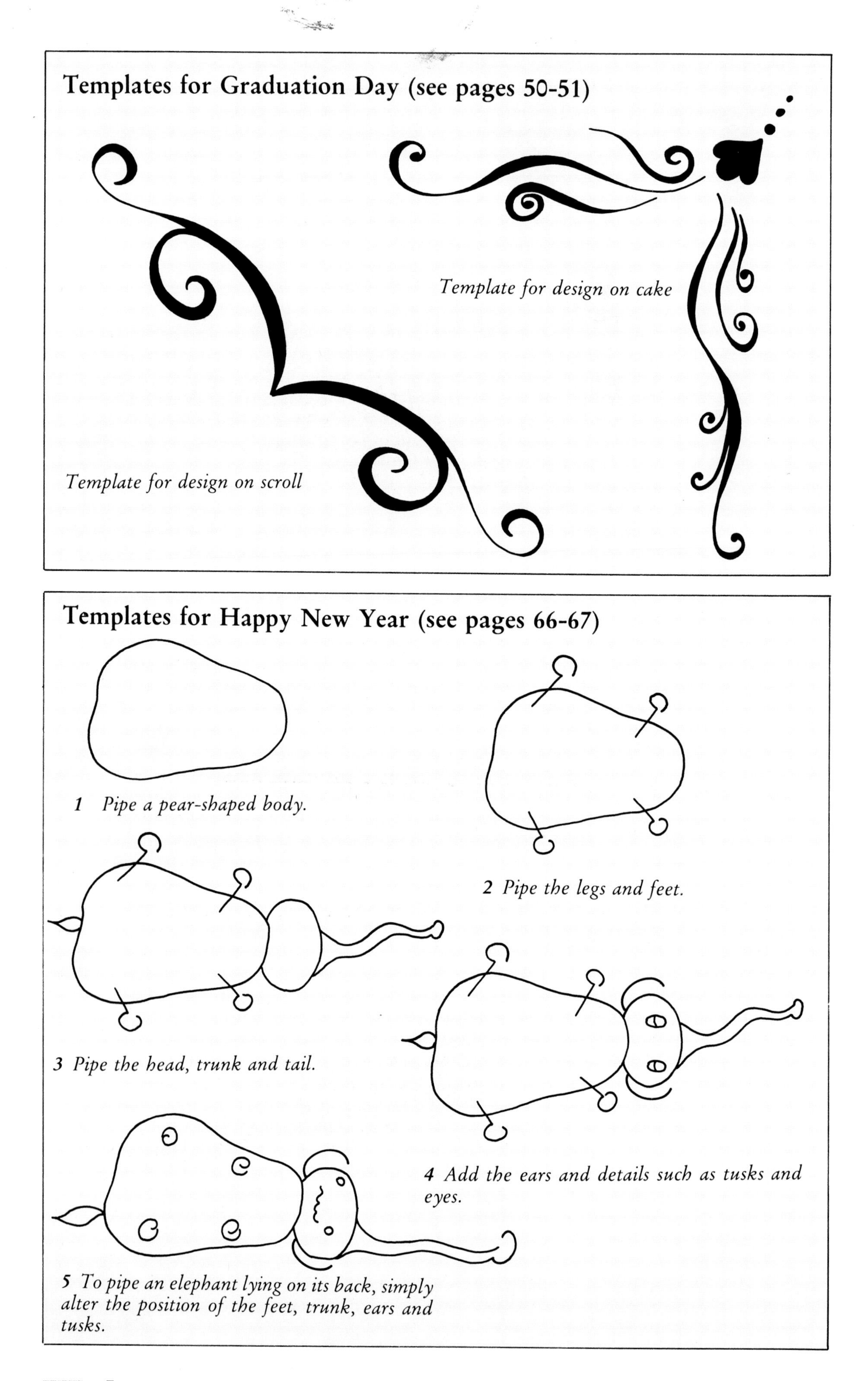

Templates for Graduation Day (see pages 50-51)

Template for design on cake

Template for design on scroll

Templates for Happy New Year (see pages 66-67)

1 Pipe a pear-shaped body.

2 Pipe the legs and feet.

3 Pipe the head, trunk and tail.

4 Add the ears and details such as tusks and eyes.

5 To pipe an elephant lying on its back, simply alter the position of the feet, trunk, ears and tusks.

PRINTED IN BELGIUM BY proost INTERNATIONAL BOOK PRODUCTION